A STUDENT'S GUIDE TO THE CORE CURRICULUM

ISI GUIDES TO THE MAJOR DISCIPLINES

GENERAL EDITOR — JEFFREY O. NELSON

EDITOR — WINFIELD J. C. MYERS

A STUDENT'S GUIDE TO PHILOSOPHY
BY RALPH M. MCINERNY

A STUDENT'S GUIDE TO LITERATURE
BY R. V. YOUNG

A STUDENT'S GUIDE TO LIBERAL LEARNING
BY JAMES V. SCHALL, S. J.

A STUDENT'S GUIDE TO THE STUDY OF HISTORY
BY JOHN LUKACS

A STUDENT'S GUIDE TO THE CORE CURRICULUM
BY MARK C. HENRIE

A STUDENT'S GUIDE TO U. S. HISTORY
BY WILFRED M. MCCLAY

A STUDENT'S GUIDE TO ECONOMICS
BY PAUL HEYNE

A STUDENT'S GUIDE TO POLITICAL PHILOSOPHY
BY HARVEY C. MANSFIELD

A Student's Guide to the Core Curriculum

MARK C. HENRIE

ISI BOOKS
WILMINGTON, DELAWARE

The Student Self-Reliance Project and the ISI Guides to the Major Disciplines are made possible by grants from the Philip M. McKenna Foundation, the Wilbur Foundation, J. Bayard Boyle, Jr., F. M. Kirby Foundation, the Huston Foundation, Castle Rock Foundation, the William H. Donner Foundation, and other contributors who wish to remain anonymous. The Intercollegiate Studies Institute gratefully acknowledges their support.

Second Printing, February 2001

Cataloging-in-Publication Data

Henrie, Mark C., 1965 -
A student's guide to the core curriculum / by Mark C. Henrie.
—1st ed.—Wilmington, Del. : ISI Books, 2000.

p. cm.

ISBN 1-882926-42-0
1. Universities and colleges—Curricula.
I. Title. II. Title: Guide to the core curriculum.

LB2361 .H46 2000 00-101235
378/.199—dc21 CIP

Published in the United States by:

ISI Books
Post Office Box 4431
Wilmington, DE 19807-0431

Cover and interior design by Sam Torode
Manufactured in Canada

CONTENTS

Introduction 1

CLASSICS DEPARTMENT:
Classical Literature in Translation 26

PHILOSOPHY DEPARTMENT:
Introduction to Ancient Philosophy 35

RELIGION DEPARTMENT:
The Bible 46

RELIGION DEPARTMENT:
Christian Thought Before 1500 54

POLITICAL SCIENCE DEPARTMENT:
Modern Political Theory 66

ENGLISH DEPARTMENT:
Shakespeare 75

HISTORY DEPARTMENT:
U. S. History Before 1865 85

HISTORY DEPARTMENT:
Nineteenth-Century European Intellectual History 94

BEYOND THE CORE:
Ten Courses More 104

STUDENT SELF-RELIANCE PROJECT:
Embarking on a Lifelong Pursuit of Knowledge? 111

INTRODUCTION

The American university has for some years been an arena for boisterous disputes about the nature of the academic enterprise and a laboratory of experimentation on a range of fundamental social questions. Some praise innovations in student life as heralding a more just and tolerant multicultural society of tomorrow. Others dismiss these innovations as representing nothing but an intrusive form of political correctness. But however we judge these controversial political matters, we all surely agree that the university is a place for education. Yet here, very often, we face a serious problem. For while the advanced research conducted at U.S. universities is the envy of the world, it is also clear that at most institutions the basic undergraduate curriculum has been neglected and consequently experienced a dissolution.

Once, American universities required all students to take an integrated sequence of courses, a core curriculum, bringing coherence to their basic studies. The core often constituted half or more of the credits required for graduation.

Through survey introductions to "the best which has been thought and said," the core sought to provide a comprehensive framework by which students could orient their more specialized studies and within which they could locate themselves.

Today however, the core has vanished or been replaced by vague distribution requirements. Students in effect are left to fend for themselves. Thus, after four years of study, all requirements fulfilled and their degrees in hand, countless students now leave college in a state of bewilderment. They sense that somehow they have been cheated, but to whom can they complain? Laudable reform efforts are sporadically undertaken on various campuses, but it may be decades before these will begin to bear fruit. In the meantime, what is a student to do?

A Student's Guide to the Core Curriculum is offered as one response to the predicament facing today's undergraduates. After a preliminary discussion of the end or *telos* of higher education, this guide directs you to the courses generally still available in university departments that may be taken as *electives* to acquire a genuine body of core knowledge. These courses provide a framework that can help you figure out what is going on in the world. Although the contemporary university has often failed in its responsibilities to its students, a motivated student can nonetheless choose his or her courses well and thus reach the goal of a liberal education.

THE IDEA OF A UNIVERSITY

All human action is done for the sake of some end. Why then do we go to college? What is our goal? What are we to *become* when we pursue an education in the liberal arts? We may encounter a variety of answers to this fundamental question, but unfortunately these answers are usually rather bad ones.

Some say that college is simply preparation for a career. But no human life is defined completely by paid employment. *Professional man*, therefore, cannot be the true end of a university education. Others champion the sophisticate's proud ability to "see through" conventional views, to critique existing society and cultivate one's individuality in the spirit of John Stuart Mill. But the subversive "why not?" which is central to such an intellectual art, actually stands rather low in the ranks of the intellectual virtues. So dogmatically *critical man* cannot be the goal of liberal education, either. And the partisans of today's multicultural diversity education proffer as their goal the amiable relativist *postmodern man*, freed of hang-ups and "beyond" critical judgment. The postmodern theorist Richard Rorty suggests we must come to understand ourselves as nothing but "clever animals." Yet this hardly seems the end of an authentically *higher* education. We must look elsewhere for an answer to our question.

John Henry Newman (1801-1890) is the philosophical soul who reflected most deeply and comprehensively about the meaning of a liberal education. Newman was probably the greatest mind, perhaps even the greatest man, of the nineteenth century; and so, to discover the true *telos* of higher education, Newman's *Idea of a University* is the place to begin.

Like today, Newman had to contend with the popular view that higher education must prove itself by a utilitarian standard, and Newman rejected that servile view. Rather, there is a *human* end, a noninstrumental end, to higher education—an end that is valued for its own sake. For Newman, the goal of a university education is always "enlargement of mind," or "illumination," or "philosophy." With none of these terms is he quite content, however. Rather, he gropes in his text for a term that may be predicated to the mind in the same way in which "health" is predicated to the body. The end of liberal education is the *health of the mind.* We desire health for what a healthy body allows us to accomplish, but also *for its own sake;* and so too with an "enlarged" or "illuminated" mind. And just as with bodies health is achieved through exercising all the parts, so, Newman claims, the health of the intellect is achieved through the broadest education possible. In Newman's historical circumstances, his educational ideal was at least partially realized in the classical curriculum of Oxford University—reading "Greats."

Newman's *Idea* offered a nontraditional defense of nineteenth-century England's traditional form of higher education.

In arguing for the value of broad and liberal learning, Newman, a Catholic priest, was in part rejecting the seminary style of education favored by his bishops. But he was also, and more pointedly, addressing the English proponents of the "scientific" style of higher education then beginning to flourish in the German universities—*Wissenschaft*. This German pedagogic regime, which was widely imitated in America in the first half of the twentieth century, had as its *telos* the production of *scientific men*, specialists in the methods of one discipline of inquiry at the expense of broader humanistic studies. Such men could, through the use of their methods, achieve ever more extensive discoveries of new knowledge, particularly in the natural sciences. Such scientific progress with its technological implications, the utilitarians were quick to note, was also very useful to society at large.

Newman's response to the partisans of specialization and *Wissenschaft* was twofold. First, he observed that while the concentrated intellectual development of the German-style scientists had perhaps a practical advantage, the cost was the narrowing, the diminishment—in fact, the partial mutilation—of the mind of each individual. No more could such specialization be recognized as intellectual health, desirable for its own sake, than could an overdeveloped right arm in an otherwise neglected body be understood as bodily health. Second, Newman insisted that a true understanding of the *whole* could be achieved only through a broad and balanced approach to the whole. The specialist, naturally impressed by the explanatory power that his discipline gives him in one narrow area of inquiry, is apt to overestimate his grasp of other matters: the nuclear scientist or the biochemist presumes to speak on moral and political questions, as if ethics is not itself a serious study with methods very unlike those of the natural sciences. In fact, Newman would argue, there is less justification for crediting the ethical judgment of a scientist who has not received a broadly liberal education—even in such debates as nuclear deterrence or cloning—than there is for crediting the judgment of a liberally educated man wholly lacking in any specialized knowledge of either science or ethics.

Lest there be any confusion, we must emphasize that Newman's arguments for broad studies are radically different from the arguments of those who champion pedagogic diversity today. The *telos* of each program differs, and this has concrete effects on the curriculum. For broad studies are, in Newman, undertaken as part of a disciplined effort to come to a view of the *whole*. Learning proceeds with the assumption that there is a unity to all knowledge, and that there is *truth* out there to be found. The mind is *opened* by the variety of studies so that it will at length *close* upon an ordered view of the *whole* that is as capacious and as rigorous as possible. "That only is true enlargement of mind which is the power of viewing many things at once as one whole," he writes. When this philosophical habit of mind is developed, "it makes every thing in some sort lead to every thing else," for a pattern or an order may thereby be discerned in the *cosmos* and in man's historical experience. Newman has precedent for this view in, for example, Thomas Aquinas, who observed that "to be wise is to establish order."

Newman continues by noting that a sheer variety of subjects of study is a necessary but not a sufficient condition for achieving illumination:

> The enlargement [of mind] consists, not merely in the passive reception into the mind of a number of ideas hitherto unknown to it, but in the mind's energetic and simultaneous action upon and towards and among those new ideas....It is the action of a formative power....it is a making the objects of our knowledge subjectively our own.... We feel our minds to be growing and expanding *then*, when we not only learn, but refer what we learn to what we know already.

If we contrast this vision with that of the multiculturalists, we see that those who educate for *postmodern man* work to "open minds" without any thought that minds might possibly close on the truth. The *absence* of truth is the point. Rather than an ordered whole, postmodern man is pure potential, pure instrumentality—and pure resignation in the face of universal chaos and flux.

For Newman, clearly, human beings can be more than mere clever animals. Indeed, Newman ultimately claims that "[t]o have even a portion of this illuminative reason and true philosophy is the highest state to which nature can aspire, in the way of intellect." Concretely, the philosophical habit of mind can be recognized in character traits such as "freedom, equitableness, calmness, moderation, and wisdom." The name Newman gives to this human achievement, the *telos* toward which liberal education aims, is the *gentleman*.

Books on the Crisis of the University

Allan Bloom's *Closing of the American Mind* (New York, 1987) did more than anything else to ignite current concerns about higher education in America. The subtitle of the work is telling: *How Higher Education Has Failed Democracy and Impoverished the Souls of Today's Students*. Bloom thought it especially important to use the word "soul" in the title, since that is what education is ultimately about. Read the first section and see if you recognize yourself.

A political and sociological account of the decline of the university was provided first by Roger Kimball's *Tenured Radicals* (New York, 1990; revised edition, 1998), which argued that countercultural radicals of the 1960s had now grown up and found their way into tenured positions in the academy; from there they pursued their utopian politics by other means. Martin Anderson's *Imposters in the Temple* (New York, 1992) makes a similar argument.

Now Newman's choice of this term, the *gentleman,* to describe the goal of liberal learning was expedient in nineteenth-century England, for its attractiveness was then reinforced by the prejudice of his time which honored a particular socioeconomic class and its habits; but Newman's intent was precisely to bring his contemporaries to re-evaluate what it was about a certain class of people that was valuable. Newman's *gentleman,* understood philosophically, is not merely a well-born, well-mannered rich man. But there *is* a connection between the manners we associate with that class of human beings and the perfected or healthy mind which a liberal education seeks to cultivate. For the properly educated man knows both what he knows and what he does not know; and consequently, he displays habits of consideration,

---

More recent works have examined the crisis of higher education by discipline: Keith Windschuttle's *The Killing of History: How Literary Critics and Social Theorists Are Murdering our Past* (New York, 1997); John Ellis's *Literature Lost: Social Agendas and the Corruption of the Humanities* (New Haven, Conn., 1997); R. V. Young's *At War with the Word: Literary Theory and Liberal Education* (Wilmington, Del., ISI Books, 1999); Victor Davis Hanson and John Heath's *Who Killed Homer? The Demise of Classical Education and the Recovery of Greek Wisdom* (New York, 1998).

The classic defense of the classical curriculum penned early in this century also rewards reading. Irving Babbitt's *Literature and the American College* (Boston, 1908; Washington, D.C., 1986) defends the pedagogic style of the small college over the research orientation of the German-style university.

courtesy, and fair-mindedness which are both moral and intellectual virtues. Moreover, there is a certain pleasing modesty to the philosophical gentleman. Because he possesses a view of the *whole*, he does not make the mistake of believing that intellectual virtue is the sole criterion of human value; the perfection of the intellect leads to the realization that intellection is not the whole of a human life.

Since today we too often associate Newman's term, *the gentleman*, with mere dilettantism, it is probably better to say that the *telos* of a liberal education is the *civilized man*. Ultimately, the reason we go to college is to become *civilized*. Does this goal inform how you are approaching your own years in college?

WESTERN CIV. AND THE GREAT BOOKS

In early twentieth-century America, when Newman's classical curriculum of Greek and Latin studies was rejected as no longer practical, certain educational leaders sought to retain the spirit of liberal learning as Newman understood it. Amidst the emergent "majors" and "electives" in the first half of the twentieth century, two models of a core curriculum were attempted. One was the "General Education" survey of Western civilization; the other was the study of the Great Books of the West. Both were noble efforts, but neither was perfect. Each tended toward a characteristic vice.

General Education in "Western Civ." was effectively a required sequence of history courses offering a unified narrative of the West. Such a core curriculum arose in American universities between the two world wars and lasted until the core was rejected in the late 1960s. This method had the advantage of providing an approach to one incarnation of the human whole, Western civilization—its art, literature, philosophy, politics, and religion—understood *as a whole*. The approach also had the advantage of locating the individual in historical time, of taking history seriously.

But the purpose of such an education was all too often self-consciously political rather than philosophical, having much to do with the perception of an ideological threat from outside the West in the form of fascism and then of communism. The universities were in effect brought into the struggle against the ideological foe by teaching students "what we are fighting for." Thus, our culture's historical narrative for the purposes of the old-fashioned "Western Civ." consisted of the story of the advance of freedom and democracy, leading to their apotheosis in contemporary America. This educational project is frequently denounced today as having been nothing but a kind of pseudocritical indoctrination into the unexamined "excellences" of one's own culture, and therefore not truly a liberal education at all. While such criticisms are often overdrawn, it is true that the history proffered in "Western Civ."

was frequently too pat. For example, the secular academics who developed "Western Civ." curricula at universities such as Columbia systematically understated the role of Christianity in Western history; and given America's wars with Germany in the first half of the twentieth century, the barbarian Gothic tribes' contribution to the "constitution of liberty" was almost completely ignored. The charge against the educational regime of "Western Civ." was ultimately that it had as its *telos* not the cultivation of the *civilized man* with a view of a genuine whole, but merely the production of the *American citizen.*

The other twentieth-century effort to retain a spirit of liberal learning in the American university was the Great Books curriculum. St. John's College in Annapolis, Maryland, is the college best known for this kind of program. In such a curriculum, certain works of literature and philosophy are read without the mediation of historical consciousness. Students are told that the first step in grappling fruitfully with such monumental works of the human mind is to attempt to understand the author as the author understood himself: to do this, students must *not* begin from the standpoint of what we know now, judging historical events negatively for their failure to measure up to our modern standards (characteristic of the Left) or else judging such events positively for their contribution to the development of our own current practices and beliefs (characteristic of the Right).

Rather, to take such texts as seriously as they deserve to be taken, we must approach them alive to the possibility that what is contained in one or the other of them may be simply *true,* and that what we modern men and women believe may be, quite simply, *false.*

In all of this, the Great Books curriculum is superior to the survey approach of "Western Civ.," for a firsthand approach to "the best which has been thought and said" educes far greater mastery of the arguments that have shaped the world. A Great Books core curriculum is as close as we come today to the education Newman championed. In order to become *civilized men,* we should make every effort to acquire an education of this sort; and insofar as current university practices and regulations frustrate this effort we have the measure of our academic corruption.

However, the Great Books approach is also given to a characteristic vice that must be carefully avoided. In their effort to avoid "indoctrination" and to convince students of the more-than-historical value of a small number of truly great books, anti-historicist defenders of those books sometimes go so far as to assert that the history of the West is not a history of "answers," but a history of *questions*—"permanent questions"—that can never have conclusive answers. Indeed, they sometimes conclude that understanding Western history as a record of such unanswerable questions is the *only* basis for believing in the West's superiority to other civilizations, which achieve their unity, it is said, around one or another set of answers. Reading the Great Books of the West in this way has as its *telos*, it is asserted, the *philosopher*—though here, the philosopher is understood in a tendentious way, owing rather more to existentialism than to older exemplars.

But to hold that all important questions remain permanently open is itself to presume, dogmatically, that history does not matter and thought does not progress. It also curiously fails to do justice to the writers of the Great Books, since these writers were without exception in the business of seeking answers and not merely engaged in thought experiments concerning questions they knew to be irresoluble. Like other practitioners of *Wissenschaft*, exponents of the Great Books too often mistake their particular skill in textual interpretation for the whole of intellectual perfection. If the "Western Civ." survey approach reduced the history of the West to the story of *freedom*, the Great Books understanding of the West as the story of *philosophy* is no less reductive. Grand as both narratives are, neither is the whole story.

What is needed in America today for the cultivation of civilized men and women is a university core curriculum exploring the West—its thought, its history, its characteristic institutions—and this curriculum should proceed largely, though not entirely, through the study of Great Books. Such a curriculum must be followed in the right spirit: not to reinforce unreflective prejudices about the superiority of one's own cultural norms, nor to achieve a spurious philosophy that privileges the activity of penetrating readers of texts. Rather, the history and the texts must be approached as disclosing the pattern of a civilization, the highest of human temporal achievements. The history and the texts must be understood as aids pointing beyond themselves to the true object of our interest—the truth of things.

A CORE OF ONE'S OWN

The American poet and memoirist William Alexander Percy wrote of his own college experience that it was designed to "unfit one for everything except the good life." Perhaps now you also want to fit yourself for nothing less than the good life—which requires coming to know what the good life is, a genuine question. Perhaps you have grown weary with the ideology and pseudosophistication that passes for higher education in so many college classrooms. And perhaps this essay has begun to convince you that there may be some wisdom to learn from, and within, our tradition. You now genuinely *want* to acquire a liberal education and become a *civilized man*. You want to achieve that philosophical habit of mind, the illumination of the reason about which Newman wrote. You want to choose the West as your own inheritance, and through that particular civilization, you want to work toward your own view of the *whole*, which is the precondition for genuine understanding. But you also want to be prepared for the "real world"—since practical concerns are part of every human life, part of the human whole, and cannot be ignored. Given all the requirements and pressures of school, how exactly do you *do* this?

Your university will likely do nothing to help you acquire the rudiments of cultural literacy. For the American academy has with very few exceptions rejected the idea of a coherent, required core curriculum in Western civilization. Harvard University long ago replaced its core curriculum with what William Bennett, the former U.S. secretary of education, has described as a "core lite"—the choice of a random assortment of courses proffering "approaches" to knowledge rather than any particular knowledge itself. The idea seems to be to hone students' minds as *instruments*, with nothing particular in their heads for those instruments to operate on—certainly no wisdom. Whether Harvard recognizes it or not, that august institution is now in the business of producing only (very) clever animals rather than civilized men and women.

But all is not lost. If you really set your mind to it, you can still acquire a genuine liberal education, even at Harvard. For in most American universities, scattered across the various departments, you can find courses that explore the central facets of the Western tradition and do so through an engagement with great texts. The trick is to find them. Your college advisor will not point you in the direction of such courses. The course catalog will not highlight them. But the courses are usually still there, waiting to be discovered. One saving grace of the contemporary university is that you have *electives*. That means you have *choices*. And with such choices comes *responsibility*.

Thus, your years of college can end up being nothing but a jumble of disconnected passing enthusiasms, leaving you in the end only confused and disappointed. Or your college years can be a time of serious intellectual growth—the springboard for genuine understanding of where we have come from and where we are going. Either way, the choice is yours. *You are now responsible for the person you will become.*

But even when you make the choice to treat your education as seriously as it deserves to be treated, how do you know where to begin? That is where this guide comes in. The following chapters are a map to guide you into the *terra incognita*, the "unknown land" that is our own civilization. Through the course of studies outlined below, you will begin to grasp the course of the West, both for good and for ill (and coming to understand what is to be praised and what is to be condemned in our history is not as easy as may first appear). You will discover whence you have come. You will begin to relate the unity and the diversity of knowledge, the one and the many. You will encounter the noble and the base. You may even recognize a wrong turn or two in our history. In choosing to devote yourself to studying the civilization of the West, you will be taking the first step to becoming a civilized man or woman.

INDISPENSABLE AIDS

Civilization, however, is not a series of entries on a college transcript. The philosophical habit of mind that recognizes connections and glimpses the pattern of the whole is something to be found not in the courses you take, but in *you*. How do you come to possess that habit, that virtue? Two things are nearly indispensable, and if you want to make the most of your college education you must actively seek them out.

The Teacher. Within all traditional cultures, the teacher is highly honored, and the obligations existing between teacher and student are a subject for deep reflection. Confucius taught that the teacher-student relationship is one of the five fundamental human forms. The teacher is understood to have something to give to the student—his wisdom—and the student in turn gives the teacher respect, gratitude, and loyalty. The formalities of such a relationship have been obscured in contemporary society. Not only are Americans less mannerly than the ancient Chinese, but we are also skeptical that anyone might actually *possess* wisdom. We tend to understand teachers more as trainers in methods of inquiry than as bearers of an *ethos*.

Nevertheless, however much this fundamental human experience has been obscured, the basic pattern can still be discerned. Each of us has had a teacher who has held a special place in our hearts, one who has shaped us in a very deep way. Years later we can recognize that we would not be the persons we are were it not for our encounter with these exceptional souls. A common mistake of college students is to believe that such intellectual mentorship ends with high school, that university students should somehow become more independent in their work. This is far from the truth. For everything that really matters in the higher learning, having a teacher remains necessary.

So by all means, seek out the good professors, the ones who care both about their subjects and about their students. And once you've found them, cultivate a relationship with them. Make use of office hours—not in search of a better grade, but to *learn* from someone who has devoted himself to the life of scholarship, someone who really is *wiser* than you, someone who can see further, if only because he is older. If you find a professor who is committed to a traditional exploration of the West and who is willing to spend time both in and outside the classroom with you, take every course you can from this professor. You will be surprised to discover how your thinking develops in response to the attention of a true teacher.

Friends. Friendship is so important that Aristotle devoted two books of his *Nicomachean Ethics* to it—and only one book to justice. One of the highest types of friendship is intellectual friendship. When you go off to college, your parents tell you to choose your friends wisely, but they have in mind keeping you away from trouble. You should choose your friends wisely, not only for the negative reason of avoiding moral hazards, but also for the positive reason that if you can

---

The Objection

"The spirit indeed is willing, but the flesh is weak." Frail creatures that we are, we seem always to be irresistibly drawn to the easier path. Thus, presented with a challenging sequence of courses that may unlock for us the history of the West, a curriculum that may transform us into civilized men and women, we are nonetheless apt to shrink from our responsibility to ourselves. When an array of easy "gut" electives seductively beckons, we acquiesce.

We then rationalize our laxity by an appeal to "hard-headed practicality." Getting ahead, getting into law school, and getting a good job all require a high grade point average, we tell ourselves. To follow a challenging course of electives may be admirable. It is what we would surely do were it not for the demands of the market, which cannot be ignored. But given these "realities," we simply cannot in good conscience thwart our own future in the romantic pursuit of such an ideal.

But here the self-justifying excuse fails. For any dean, any law school

find your way into a group of serious intellectual friends, you will learn immensely more than if you try to "go it alone." Indeed, such friendships will change your life.

Too often in American university life we find a shocking anti-intellectualism, even at the most prestigious schools. The young of every age and time face distractions such as the lure of the opposite sex, but in our time the distractions have grown relentlessly: television, video games, sports, extracurricular activities. Surely we are the most *entertained* people in history. But entertainment is not education. Intellectual friendship is the surest means for connecting pleasure with true education.

---

admissions officer, and any employer will tell you—and tell you truly—that grades are not the only thing that matters on a transcript. When you leave college for the next step in your life, the quality of your course of studies will be scrutinized to determine how serious you are. Employers will also want to know how broad your learning is and therefore how capable you are of continuing to learn throughout your life, an absolute necessity in a fast-changing world. Thus, a student who can show that he has set for himself, independently, a rigorous course of studies in Western civilization and who has seen this project through to the end has a distinct advantage in the market. Even if his grades suffer somewhat, such a student has something to say for himself in a cover letter or in an admissions essay that others do not. He is the better candidate for jobs and for graduate school admissions. Viewed strictly from the standpoint of "hard-headed practicality," then, the student who pursues his own core curriculum in the Western tradition has a future that is more, not less, secure.

The objection, in other words, is an entirely false one.

Beyond distractions, however, an anti-intellectual attitude to the life of the mind is evident even in some of those who work most diligently at their courses. For Americans have learned a habit of work and leisure that is hostile to the intellectual life. Probably owing to America's Puritan foundations, we tend to understand leisure as the absence of work. The ancients, however, understood work as the absence of leisure. Leisure (*otium*, in Latin) was the substantial thing, and work the negation or absence of that (*negotium*). The ancients understood that human beings were made to *enjoy* their leisure seriously: the serious use of leisure is the cultivation of the mind, which is pleasant and good for its own sake. Americans, however, approach university studies as "work," as *negotium*, from which, once the work is done, they are "freed." Free time, such as time spent with friends, is thus kept clean of any trace of the learning of the classroom. This is no way to learn. It isn't even any real way to enjoy yourself.

In the everyday course of intellectual friendship, friends share with each other their moments of insight, present them to each other for testing. Such moments in turn require us to reconsider not just that discrete matter, but everything else in our view of the whole that touches upon the matter. For example, in a conversation about feminism, someone observes that women in recent decades have been treated with greater justice, but that they are also probably less happy. The mind races at such a striking formulation. Is that true? How can justice and happiness conflict? If they do, which is to be preferred? As Socrates knew twenty-five centuries ago, the normal means for penetrating further and synthesizing our knowledge is *dialogue*. Intellectual friendship consists in a great ocean of dialogue and discussion, and those who have tasted it know it is among the highest human pleasures.

So, seek out as friends people who are in the habit of asking questions, even ridiculous questions, and who are willing in turn to share their moments of insight with you. Then you will use your four years of leisure well; just as a true teacher, a true intellectual friendship will inevitably change your life.

THE CURRICULUM

Finally, there is the very practical matter of which courses to select. Most likely, your university will already require courses in the sciences and a foreign language. This is all for the good. In order for you to understand both the power and the limits of natural science—which is the privileged way of knowing in our time—it is important to experience the working of the sciences at first hand. Moreover, while it is devilishly difficult for Americans to learn foreign languages, the struggle really does pay off, if you keep at it, with genuine enlargement of mind. The common saying is actually true: Some thoughts are best expressed in certain languages rather than others. To acquire a foreign language thus opens up, potentially, an entirely new world to you. So take these requirements seriously.

To assemble the elective core curriculum outlined in this guide, then, the Intercollegiate Studies Institute examined course catalogs of public and private colleges and universities, both large and small, from every region in the country. We also consulted literally dozens of distinguished academics in various disciplines. These professors were asked how they would craft a core curriculum aiming to introduce students to the complexities of the Western tradition and to the spirit of liberal learning. These professors were united in their preference for courses emphasizing primary texts and, conversely, in their recommendation that survey courses should generally be avoided. Direct engagement with great books has all the benefits previously described, while students in a survey course are too easily held hostage to a professor's opinions, because they lack any textual basis for challenging him. That is no small difficulty in today's academy.

The eight courses described here (one course each semester in a four-year college career) are generally available in the departmental offerings of most universities in the United States. In each of the following chapters, you will read about how the course content fits into a sophisticated understanding of the West. You will also be given tips for how to get the most out of the course at your school. And secondary reading is suggested in the event that your professors are offering politicized lectures.

While neither this nor any curriculum is entirely comprehensive, this do-it-yourself core curriculum does allow you to encounter much of the history of the West, and to do so from a variety of perspectives. With this curriculum, taken on your own, you have a real opportunity to leave college after four years not just with a diploma but also with *understanding*.

CLASSICAL LITERATURE IN TRANSLATION

THE FRENCH WRITER Charles Péguy once observed that "Homer is ever new; nothing is as old as the morning paper." One of the best reasons for studying the works of the oldest of dead white European males is their very novelty. Moreover, in reading the literature of ancient Greece and Rome, you are engaging the same texts that influenced virtually every educated person in our history. So if you want to understand the mind of Descartes or Abraham Lincoln or William Faulkner or even Clint Eastwood—and if you want to understand yourself—you need to understand the classics.

Virtually every university's classics department offers an introductory course of classical literature in translation that will cover both the *Iliad* and the *Odyssey*. There will also be a few tragic plays, often Sophocles' *Antigone* or something from the *Oedipus* cycle, and if you are lucky, a comedy or two, such as Aristophanes' *Lysistrata* or else *The Clouds*. Many universities have separate introductory Greek and Roman literature courses, but most will combine the two by covering at least the great classic of Roman literature: Virgil's *Aeneid.*

❧

The story of the West begins with a story. The blind bard, Homer (c. 8th century B.C.), recited tales so compelling that they seized the Greek imagination for centuries. Homer's *Iliad* is the story of a fair young warrior, Achilles, who takes the leading role in the defeat of a great and ancient city, Troy. Achilles is one ideal of the Greeks. The Greeks were conscious that theirs was a "youthful" civilization. They knew that they inhabited a world in which there existed more ancient civilizations such as Egypt and Persia, and also a world in which civilizations had risen and fallen, such as that of the Minoans—and that the Greeks were implicated in that fall. In Plato's dialogue *Timaeus,* an Egyptian priest says to the lawgiver of Athens, "O Solon, Solon, you Greeks are always children, and there is no Greek who is an old man. You are all young in your souls, and you have in them no old belief handed down by ancient tradition, nor any knowledge that is hoary with age." The Greek spirit was one of youthfulness; they were parvenus in a world that valued the wisdom of age. Consequently, there is a remarkable freshness to Greek writing, and that is a freshness that continues to define the West.

Moreover, Achilles is *not* the leader of the Greek forces—

Agamemnon is—and this is important. Achilles is one of many lesser warlords, though certainly the greatest in skill at arms. That at the origin of Western literature lies the story of an exemplary *individual* who is *not* the paramount ruler sets the West apart from other civilizations whose most ancient and formative literatures are accounts of the exemplary and seemingly effortless acts of emperors or gods.

In the *Iliad*, we also see something else peculiar to Western thought: a sympathetic treatment of the enemy, especially the valiant Trojan Hector, who is perhaps the noblest character in the entire epic. The most touching scenes of domestic happiness are portrayed in the doomed city of Troy; the realization that all this will be put to fire and the sword moves us, as it moved the ancient Greeks, to sorrow for their adversaries.

The *Iliad* is about the *wrath* of Achilles: "Tell, Muse, of the wrath of Achilles" is the epic's first line. This anger, which is the root of the great warrior's courage, and therefore of his heroism, proves to be the hero's undoing. This is man's tragic circumstance: whatever his excellences, man cannot escape the limits of his existence. Indeed, all the heroes of the *Iliad* find themselves trapped by their situation and the roles they are called upon by tradition to play. The *Iliad*, however, culminates in an unusual act of magnanimity on Achilles' part: perhaps there is a way for man to "defeat" fate? The *Iliad* is thus the story of a hero contending against the limits of human nature, at least as he knows that nature reflected through the myths of the Greek world. The poem asks, in effect, What is possible for man? What may he hope for? And can he live with the truth of his state? These are questions that are as important for every one of us today as they were to the Greeks more than twenty-five centuries ago.

The companion epic to the *Iliad* is the *Odyssey*, a more entertaining read and the story of another hero—Odysseus—and his wandering search for *home* after the end of the Trojan War. Viewed together, the Homeric epics are a meditation on the human condition. Is the human condition, the human "homeland," fundamentally that of the *Iliad?* Are we all, effectively, naturally, in a world of strife and war? Are we "made" for war? Or is humanity's true home the world of the hearth, of the domestic life of peace—the goal of Odysseus in the *Odyssey?* Or are we natural wanderers, wayfarers? And what is *best* in life—the glory of military victory, or the quiet happiness of family life, or something else? The question of the best life is a very Greek one, which might lead us to ask why it is a question we hardly ever ask today.

The *Iliad* ends tragically while the *Odyssey* ends comically. These may be the two limiting extremes of human experience, and therefore of poetic invention—or perhaps not. In either event, Greek drama soon afterward developed both genres. Tragedy came first, and comedy followed; and that sequence is significant. For the tragic sensibility depends on man's intuition of his own greatness in collision with human limitation, particularly the limit of fate. But Greek comedy emerged with a sudden doubt about the greatness of man. Perhaps man is really a ridiculous creature? If so, it is best not to probe too deeply into his condition. The comic playwright penning his most scatological scenes is in reality issuing a cautionary warning.

Ultimately, attending carefully to the Greeks should lead us to understand both our similarities with *and* our differences from the oldest dead white European males. A great mistake of cultivated minds throughout our history has been to overemphasize continuity. Nineteenth-century Englishmen read their Greeks and found in Athens a culture of proper gentlemen. A well-raised Englishman, it was contended, could have walked into Periclean Athens and felt deeply at home. Germans of the same period read their Greeks and found the romantic souls of German *Volk*. Today, some find the Greeks to be the fathers of a bourgeois liberalism not unlike modern America. There is an element of truth in each of these characterizations, but none is true simply.

❦

Ever since the Renaissance, a bias against the Romans has prevailed among the learned. The Romans' legal, political, military, architectural, and engineering accomplishments are admittedly great, but what of their philosophy and their art? Derivative of the Greeks, it is said. Yet Virgil's epic, the *Aeneid*, is both an imitation of Homer and also something quite new. We see this in the very first line of the poem. In Homer's epics, the *Muse* sings out. But Virgil's *Aeneid* begins with the line, "I sing of arms and a man...." *I* sing. That is new. And for Virgil, the *destiny* of pious Aeneas is not quite the *fate* of the Homeric heroes. A close comparison of the *Aeneid* with the *Iliad* shows how Virgil (70-19 B.C.) grapples with the Homeric tradition so as to surpass it, and it is this engagement with tradition that led T. S. Eliot to name the *Aeneid* "the classic of all Europe."

One of the best reasons to read the *Aeneid* is that it will disabuse you of a silly notion you may have picked up in high school English classes. Namely, the opinion that what literature is fundamentally about is the struggle of the individual with society. A bright student is apt to get this impression in large part because the works commonly found in high school curricula are designed to connect with young people who are coming to understand and define their individuality. But much great art has nothing to do with this theme. And there is probably no better example than the *Aeneid*, an epic that was actually commissioned by the Emperor Augustus as political propaganda, and in which the hero is individuated by his *service* to society. In the *Aeneid*, we might even say that we find represented that classical ideal against which all the rebellious American high school literature is aimed.

❧

What can you expect from your professor in the typical introductory classics course? The older generation of classics professors are among the finest members of the academy. The rigor of their language studies and the quality of the texts they have pored over for years have made them perhaps curmudgeonly, but also deeply humane. Not infrequently, however, the younger generation of classicists have learned all the worst habits of postmodern literary critics. You should become suspicious when a professor begins to use code words and catch phrases such as the "social construction of homosexuality" or "retrieving women's experience." Since any great work of literature contains an entire *world*, it is a gross reduction to view that world through the narrowing lens of sex or gender.

The principal error that beginners in the study of literature encounter is that their professors' interpretations of the text, so powerfully presented in expert lectures, overwhelm students so that they can then not really see other possibilities for interpreting and understanding. Despite themselves, students then parrot the professor's line. A good way to combat this natural tendency is to consult several editions or translations of the text and *read the introductions*. Very frequently these introductions are written by some of the finest literary minds—and if they have any biases, the best way to observe them is to read other introductions.

The literature on classical literature is vast, and your library is filled with marvelous introductions to the ancient writers. Cedric Whitman was the author of some of the best works on classical themes in the tradition of the New Criticism, the critical tradition that examines poems as integral pieces of art. Whitman's *Homer and the Heroic Tradition* (Cambridge, Mass., 1958) is an excellent introduction to the *Iliad* and the *Odyssey*, and his *Aristophanes and the Comic Hero* (Cambridge, Mass., 1964) discusses the major themes and plays of that poet. Bernard Knox, *The Heroic Temper: Studies in Sophoclean Tragedy* (Berkeley, Calif., 1964; reprinted, 1983) provides a powerful reading of tragedy similar to that of Whitman.

For other views, Jasper Griffin's *Homer on Life and Death* (Oxford, 1980) is an example of the best of traditional scholarship developed in a life of teaching undergraduates. Louise Cowan's *Terrain of Comedy* (Dallas, 1984) includes a wise interpretation of Aristophanes.

T. S. Eliot's essay "Vergil and the Christian World," in his book *On Poetry and Poets* (New York, 1957), contains the thoughts of the greatest English-language poet of the twentieth century on the classic of Roman civilization. C. S. Lewis's *Preface to Paradise Lost* (London, 1942) contains an excellent chapter on the *Aeneid* as well. For more extended treatment, Brooks Otis's *Virgil: A Study in Civilized Poetry* (Oxford, 1964) is a penetrating study of the *Aeneid* and other works.

If you want to understand the social institutions of the Homeric age, M. I. Finley's *World of Odysseus* (New York, 1954; second edition, 1979) attempts to uncover the historical facts of life of an age so different from our own. *The Oxford History of the Classical World*, edited by John Boardman, Jasper Griffin, and Oswyn Murray (Oxford, 1986), is likewise a reliable source of such information. For a philosophical view of the meaning of classical civilization in general, Eric Voegelin's *World of the Polis* (Baton Rouge, La., 1957), while difficult, is illuminating.

INTRODUCTION TO ANCIENT PHILOSOPHY

HAVING TASTED the wisdom of the classical poets, you'll discover something unsettling quite soon in a course on ancient philosophy: virtually every Greek play and countless lines of Homer would have been censored, banished from the ideal political community described in Plato's great work of political philosophy, the *Republic.* Plato's teacher, Socrates (c. 469-399 B.C.), the famous gadfly of Athens condemned to drink poisonous hemlock for corrupting the young men of his city, appears in the *Republic* spiritedly arguing against the poetry of the Greeks, for he believes that such poetry is *corrupting.* Very early in the Western tradition, we already see powerful arguments against the "traditional" curriculum. Such a tradition of examining tradition is one of the signal achievements of the West.

That most ironical philosopher, Socrates, is the one who "brought philosophy down from the heavens and into the city," according to Cicero. Before Socrates, philosophers sought to understand the workings of *nature* (*physis* in Greek)—biology, physics, the motions of the heavens. Socrates, by contrast, turned his attention to man and the meaning of his existence; he sought to uncover the unchanging *nature* of man. In his philosophizing, Socrates opposed a group known as Sophists, who focused their intellectual energies not on the heavens or on man but on lawyerly expertise in rhetoric so as to control the political assemblies of the Greek cities. In effect, the Sophists seem to have held the opinion that there are no universal truths to be found in human affairs, all is relative, and so the only thing worth knowing about human affairs is how to manipulate them: the point of learning, for the Sophists, was not wisdom but power. Socrates was the great critic of the Sophists, a *philosopher* or *lover of wisdom* (rather than of power).

Philosophy is sometimes called "Socratism"—Nietzsche called it that—so crucial was Socrates to our understanding of what philosophy is. And it is recorded that Socrates believed that philosophy is something that cannot be written down. Philosophy for Socrates was not some set of asserted doctrines but rather a *way of life*, a life of constant questioning in the quest to determine that which *is*. Conversation is thus the central philosophical activity. This is why Plato (427-347 B.C.), who did write down a philosophy, did so in the form of dialogues, which are rather like small dramas or plays.

But whereas poets such as Homer or Sophocles seek to *re*present the human condition, to *display* it in all its concrete variety, philosophers are driven by the thought that what we "see," what we *think* we "know" about the world around us, is in some way a mask or an illusion. Philosophers seek to penetrate behind appearances to grasp what is "really real" both in nature and in human nature. For instance, faced with the many differing customs of men in different cities, Socrates did not conclude, as the Sophists did, that all is relative in human affairs. Rather, he redoubled his efforts to discover the unchanging human *nature* behind or within such customs.

At the heart of Plato's *Republic*, Socrates recounts the famous analogy of the cave. In this tale, a group of men have been chained down since birth and forced to watch puppet-shadows playing on their cave wall. These chained men are like us, Socrates says, but we know that this is true only when we are freed and dragged out of the cave, where we can see the truth of things by the light of the sun. Another fundamental contention of all ancient philosophy is, then, that philosophy is the road to liberation, for only by philosophy can we discover *what is*—including the life that is best by nature. In this course, you just might experience that Socratic liberation for yourself.

❧

In your readings you will first encounter Plato's meditation on the trial of Socrates, the *Apology*, which most directly discusses the philosophical way of life. What does it mean to be a philosopher? Why is the philosopher necessarily a *problem* for the political community? And is the philosopher's life really the best life? The *Crito* and the *Phaedo* then recount the last days of Socrates after his trial and before his execution. These dialogues examine Socrates' political obligation and his thoughts about the soul and the afterlife: philosophy, it seems, is really about learning to *die*.

Plato's other dialogues each address a particular fundamental question. In the *Meno*, we see what the Platonic Socrates understands as knowledge. True knowledge is like a geometrical proof: once it is known, we can't imagine not having known it all along. It is as if we "remembered" this knowledge, though we had never learned it. To know the properties of an isosceles triangle is truer knowledge than to know who won the Battle of Waterloo, for the properties of an isosceles triangle cannot but be. The philosopher wants all his knowledge to be as demonstrable as that, which is why the gate of Plato's Academy bore an inscription warning away anyone ignorant of geometry.

Another characteristically Platonic observation about the philosophical life is the important role of love or desiring—

of *eros*. In the *Phaedrus*, the Platonic Socrates describes the erotic element of the philosophical quest in the most powerful way, while the *Symposium* recounts a drinking party with a long and sometimes ribald conversation about love. What is love *for*? Is love good for us? Should we seek to minimize our loves so as to achieve autonomy? These are questions that young men and women naturally wonder about today; they are questions that all human beings must ask, and that all human beings answer in the way they live their lives. Perhaps you will find wisdom in Plato's answers.

The *Republic*, Plato's greatest work, is too complex to describe briefly, but you must keep in mind while reading it that the "politics" of the *Republic* is recounted only in answer to a question about where virtue might reside in the human soul. The *Republic* is a book about the soul. There is actually more attention given to politics as such in the *Gorgias*, which contains the strongest Platonic arguments against the Sophists. Not the least interesting aspect of the *Gorgias* is Plato's depiction of the Sophist Callicles, who is nothing less (or more) than a Nietzschean more than twenty centuries before the fact.

❧

It is almost impossible not to be swept up in the philosophical enthusiasm of Plato. His dialogues are a *joy* to read. Unfortunately, it is more difficult for many students to sustain that interest with Plato's greatest student, Aristotle (384-322 B.C.). Aristotle's works are not dialogues but treatises (perhaps even the notes of his lecture courses) that aim to be complete accounts of every possible subject of inquiry. His goal is apparent when we list his titles: *Politics*, *Rhetoric*, *Poetics*, *Physics*, *On the Generation of Animals*, *On the Heavens*, etc. Moreover, whereas Plato is suspicious of appearances and seeks to reach knowledge as certain as a geometric proof, Aristotle is more empirically minded. He too wants to discover *what is*, but he begins his scientific and philosophical inquiries with *observation*. If geometry is the paradigmatic science for Plato, biology seems to be the paradigmatic science for Aristotle. In other words, what is most striking about the *cosmos* to Aristotle is that it contains biological entities, including man.

Most students will profit most immediately from the *Nicomachean Ethics*. Here, Aristotle asks, what is the virtue (*arête*, which means, literally, *excellence*) of a human being? If an excellent knife is one that cuts well, what is an excellent man? Aristotle tries to answer that question completely, describing in the process both moral and intellectual virtues and discussing the importance of friendship for a good human life. What will be most striking for many students is Aristotle's insistence that the moral life aims at *eudaemonia*, the complete happiness of the person. The reason to act morally, the reason to develop virtuous habits, the reason to cultivate the soul is to be *happy.*

Plato's *Republic* is a book about the soul, but Aristotle presents his views on this subject directly, in the work *De Anima (On the Soul).* For Aristotle, plants, animals, and human beings all have souls, but ascending up from plants to humans, the soul at each stage acquires something not available to the lower form. The human soul is one of the strangest things in the cosmos, and Aristotle finds himself ultimately unable to give a coherent account of it. His perplexity in *De Anima* will be resolved in different ways by later Christian theologians and by Jewish and Islamic philosophers.

You will likely also be required to grapple with at least parts of the *Categories*, the *Physics*, and the *Metaphysics*, which are all difficult works, requiring the guidance of a skilled professor. But do not think for a minute that even the most abstruse points of Aristotelian metaphysics are not relevant! On the contrary, how we imagine the basic structure of reality decisively informs how we may understand God, the self, and human ethics, among other rather relevant concerns. Moreover, Aristotle's account of the basic structure of reality may be *true*. If so, we'll all have to reassess something we've been taught to view as simple fact: atomism.

As early as elementary school, we learn of modern science's

heroic quest for the "fundamental building blocks" of matter—the atoms. We soon learn that atoms are composed of even smaller particles: protons, neutrons, and electrons. And if we read popular scientific literature or take physics courses in college, we discover that protons and neutrons are themselves composed of smaller particles, quarks. But here we begin to learn that these tiniest particles are extremely strange; indeed, they hardly exist at all, which is odd indeed for a "fundamental building block." What we do not learn in all this is that the quest for the smallest bits of matter represents a prior commitment by modern science to one of the metaphysical views of ancient philosophy: atomism. From before the time of Socrates, atomism was a good contender for a "Theory of Everything." Atomism, however, was explicitly rejected by Aristotle in favor of his account of substances composed of form and matter. Today's speculative physics has turned up results that raise questions about the adequacy of any kind of atomism, results that seem rather more consistent with Aristotle. Even metaphysics can be very interesting indeed!

Political correctness may creep into discussions of the *political* philosophy of Plato and Aristotle. Plato is an explicit "elitist" of the first order, and Aristotle gives an account of "natural slaves." Aristotle's discussion of women may raise eyebrows as well. The fact that our intuitions about human equality differ so markedly from those of Plato and Aristotle is significant, and we should certainly consider how and why these differences exist. But we should take care to examine the ancient arguments first and not simply dismiss them out of hand.

But the more pressing problem in ancient philosophy courses is a tendency for some professors to apply modern analytic techniques to the ancient texts, and thus to find them logically wanting—nothing but "brilliant errors." What is compelling and true in the vision of the ancients does not concern these professors. When a course in ancient philosophy is approached merely for historical interest, it can easily become rather boring, and rightly so. What is always important in any philosophical study is to remain open to the possibility of discovering truth, and nothing can dim this prospect more than a professor who himself finds unconvincing the philosophy he is teaching.

If you find your philosophy professor uninspiring, therefore, you might want to talk to a classics professor or to a professor of political science who teaches ancient political theory. Either might provide the inspiration that the philosophy department might lack. (However, the texts you read in the philosophy department's standard introductory course provide the most representative sampling of ancient philosophy.)

As for supplemental reading, it is no exaggeration to say that Plato is the best introduction to Plato. Try first to read him without the mediation of secondary literature. Still, Mary Nichols's *Socrates and the Political Community* (Albany, N.Y., 1987) is engagingly written and will entice you into genuinely philosophical reading. F. M. Cornford's *Before and After Socrates* (Cambridge, 1932) is always in print and provides good background on Greek philosophy in general. *The Republic: The Odyssey of Philosophy*, by Jacob Howland (New York, 1993), is a brief reading of Plato's great dialogue in relation to the broader Greek literary tradition. Robert E. Cushman's *Therapeia: Plato's Conception of Philosophy* (Chapel Hill, N.C., 1958; Westport, Conn., 1976) is a thorough treatment of Plato's central teaching: that the practice of the philosophic life entails a radical reorientation—indeed a conversion—of the person toward the Good. In addition, *The Sophists,* by W. K. C. Guthrie (London, 1971), presents those pre-Socratics in the most dispassionate light.

Mortimer Adler was an enthusiastic popularizer of Aristotle's thought, and his *Aristotle for Everybody: Difficult Thought Made Easy* (New York, 1978) is extremely accessible, so it is a good place to begin. Jonathan Lear's *Aristotle: The Desire to Understand* (Cambridge, 1988) is an advanced overview of Aristotle's complete works, while Terence Irwin's *Aristotle's First Principles* (Oxford, 1988) is a discrete work of philosophy treating Aristotle's first principles first. *The Cambridge Companion to Aristotle*, Jonathan Barnes, ed. (Cambridge, 1995), contains a variety of solid contemporary essays.

The articles on "Plato" and "Aristotle" in *History of Political Philosophy*, Leo Strauss and Joseph Cropsey, eds. (Chicago, 1963; third edition, 1987), are very sophisticated introductions to the political dimension of these thinkers, but tend to slight their broader philosophical contributions. Eric Voegelin's *Plato and Aristotle* (Baton Rouge, La., 1957) is a monumental introduction to both great minds with particular attention paid to the religious dimension of their thought. Finally, Giovanni Reale's *History of Ancient Philosophy*, translated by John Catan (Albany, N.Y., 1985), has a volume devoted to Plato and Aristotle.

THE BIBLE

THE *nature* or *physis* that is the subject of inquiry for the classical philosophers is by definition that which cannot but be. If something cannot but be, it must always have existed, since nothing can come from nothing. Consequently, in the vision of classical philosophy, the cosmos is "pre-eternal." The cosmos cannot have had a beginning, nor can it have an end. Insofar as there was any Greek philosophy of history, therefore, it necessarily considered history in terms of cycles. Just as nature has cycles, the seasons, so have the affairs of men. In principle, there can be nothing genuinely *new* under the sun. The ancient philosophers were therefore wholly unprepared for the advent of *revealed religion*, and in particular for the incarnation of the Son of God, the Christian revelation. The Gospel, the "good news," is, precisely, *new.*

Christianity changed the world more profoundly than anything ever had or has, and nothing so defines Western thought and practice as the legacy of Christianity. For the believer, Christ's life, death, and resurrection open up nothing less than the only way to salvation, which is eternal life with God. But even without the eyes of faith, the litany of developments generally understood as peculiar to the Christian world is striking: the rise of companionate marriage and the equality of the sexes, the abolition of slavery, an emphasis on the individual and his rights, the separation of church and state, hospitals, universities, and the list goes on. Even modern science can be seen as requiring a Christian intellectual background, for modern science is closely tied to a technological desire to intervene in the natural world, and a belief in the possibility of technological progress is itself only possible if time is understood as *linear* rather than *cyclical*, a thought that is introduced by the revealed religions.

But perhaps it is in everyday personal judgments that the West's Christian heritage is most striking, yet least remarked upon. Consider, for example, the highest moral virtue according to Aristotle: *megalopsychia* or magnanimity—"greatsouledness." This is the virtue of one who takes for himself the honor due him. In other words, something like justified pride is the highest moral virtue for Aristotle. How different this is from Christ's teaching in the Beatitudes—that those who are poor in spirit are blessed, and that the meek shall inherit the earth. How different this is from the Christian humility that acknowledges that any excellence we might possess is a gift from God. How different, in other words, is Aristotle's moral view from ours, even when we aren't believers.

The Muslims refer to Muslims, Christians, and Jews as "People of the Book." All three faiths are unlike Eastern religions in that they are constituted by a revelation of the will of a transcendent God in historical time. But Christianity is also unique, for unlike Moses or Muhammad, Jesus Christ did not come in order to write down a new law. While Jews and Muslims revere their scriptures as the Word of God delivered by patriarchs and prophets, for Christians, Christ was himself "the Word [of God] made flesh." Christ does not *write;* he *is* and he *acts*. Still, for nearly twenty centuries the men and women of the West have found the meaning of their collective and personal existence revealed in the text of the Christian Bible, and no liberal education is complete without an encounter with that Word.

Some religion departments offer a combined introductory course on the Old and New Testaments called "The Bible." Others offer only two separate courses—one on "The Hebrew Bible" (the Old Testament), the other on "The Christian Scriptures" (the New Testament). A course on the whole Bible is preferable, but if you must choose between the Old and New Testaments, opt for the New. For the Christian revelation recorded in the New Testament has served decisively as the lens through which the West has understood the whole Word of God, including that Word recorded in the Old Testament. Besides, if Christ is he who the Christians claim he is, then he is not simply a new kind of hero, greater than either Achilles or Socrates; he is the central axis of all history. Any encounter with this remarkable person must begin, of course, with the New Testament.

Perhaps the saddest fact about the modern (secular) American university is that the standard course offered on the Bible is among the most corrupt and corrupting in the curriculum. Countless college students have lost their faith by studying the Bible in college. The reason for this is the virtually universal acceptance by academic biblical scholars in the modern university of the "historical-critical method," an approach to Scripture study that may be traced to German liberal Protestantism in the nineteenth century.

Essentially, the practitioners of this method of biblical interpretation assert that the biblical text is only "explained" when one has explained the historical situation in which the text was written and to which the text apparently responds. Whereas in Christian tradition the Scriptures were understood to have several layers of meaning—a nuanced approach—for the historical critics, the "real" meaning of the text is to be found only in historical context—which is known definitively, of course, only by the historical critics themselves. Needless to say, theirs is not a subtle approach to the Bible.

Armed with their method, academic biblical critics like to pronounce upon the "misinterpretations" of the Christian churches through the centuries. Eventually they come to such absurdities as the so-called Jesus Seminar, whose members regularly vote on which sayings of Jesus recorded in the Gospels are authentic and which were, well, *made up* by the Gospel writers. The historical critics are perhaps the first deconstructionists, rejecting the *authority* of the biblical text and understanding it instead as the outcome of contending forms of political *power*. But in giving their highly speculative (and often simply fanciful) accounts of how the biblical text came to be, these critics have nothing really useful to say about the reception and interpretation of the canonized text in the centuries-long tradition of believers.

The good news in biblical studies today is that devastating objections have been raised against the historical-critical method. The skepticism that the historical critics wielded so vigorously against traditional faith has now been directed against the tradition of historical criticism itself. The project of historical criticism can now be seen as a pristine example of the Enlightenment effort to displace what it understood to be unreflective "tradition" with an absolute "science" arrived at by open-minded, autonomous, or neutral inquiry. As with so many of the Enlightenment's projects, historical critics' own prior ideological commitments and generally intolerant closed-mindedness are now increasingly clear. Faced with such new post-Enlightenment perspectives, the historical critics must now admit that their submerged intellectual premises frequently have made their interpretative arguments perfectly circular: their secularizing conclusions were implicit in their secular assumptions, which are in no sense either "autonomous" or "neutral." With the emergence of a younger generation of biblical scholars who have absorbed these critiques, the Jesus Seminar, the apogee of the historical critical enterprise, now seems an embarrassment to the historical critics themselves.

In secular American universities, the history of biblical studies we have described above means that you are more likely to find a genuinely open-minded view of traditional biblical interpretations among the *younger* faculty. That said, however, for believers, it is still best to take a course on the Bible only after they have situated themselves on campus religiously: that is, made contact with an ecclesial community, whether a church or a para-church group, and come to know a clergyman who may be consulted when difficulties or doubts arise. In the end, for the Bible to be read and understood as Sacred Scripture, it must be read with the mind of the community of faith. A local church group or clergyman will also be familiar with the quality of the course offered in your university's religion department. In large cities, they may also know of better Bible courses offered in nearby seminaries which are *not* dominated by the historical-critical method. Such courses may often be taken for easily transferable credit. Sometimes there is also a professor in a university's faculty who would be willing to supervise an independent study of the Bible. This is another way to investigate this indispensable book without the glib reductionism of the historical critics.

❧

There are numerous books you can consult that will help you judge the persuasiveness of the arguments of the historical critics. Mark Powell's *Jesus as a Figure in History* is a textbook offering balanced critiques of the major historical-critical schools from a mildly evangelical Protestant perspective. More polemical is Luke Timothy Johnson's *Real Jesus* (San Francisco, 1996). The book's subtitle, *The Misguided Quest for the Historical Jesus and the Truth of the Traditional Gospels*, sums up its message. I. H. Marshall's *New Testament Interpretation: Essays on Principles and Methods* (Exeter, 1977; revised edition, 1985) is a very sound exploration of the topic from an evangelical viewpoint. William R. Farmer and Denis Farkasfalvy provide an excellent and accessible discussion of redaction questions in *The Formation of the New Testament Canon: An Ecumenical Approach* (New York, 1983).

For questions about authorship of the books of the Old Testament, see Umberto Cassuto, *The Documentary Hypothesis and the Composition of the Pentateuch: Eight Lectures* translated by Israel Abrahams (Jerusalem, 1961), which is an elegant response to liberal and secularizing scholarship.

To get a sense for the many-faceted ways in which Christians in the first centuries understood the biblical message, you may want to consult the series, *Ancient Christian Commentary on Scripture* (Downers Grove, Ill., 1998-1999). These volumes collect statements by the Fathers of the Church on particular passages in the biblical books. Frequently, the statements are taken from sermons, and so there is an immediacy and practicality evident that you may find refreshing yet perhaps strangely familiar. *A Commentary on the Gospels* (London, 1952) by Ronald Knox, who is famous for his translation of the Bible, is also an elegant, sophisticated explication of the New Testament from the Catholic perspective.

If you are not a believer, and you find discussions of redaction and hypothetical source documents baffling, try N. T. Wright's *The Challenge of Jesus: Rediscovering Who Jesus Was & Is* (Downers Grove, Ill., 1999). You might even try C. S. Lewis's famous work *Mere Christianity* (New York, 1952; London, 1998) to see what all the fuss is about.

CHRISTIAN THOUGHT BEFORE 1500

BELIEVING STUDENTS perturbed by the contentions of the historical critics of the Bible would be heartened to read the *Contra Celsum* of Origen of Alexandria (A.D. 185-254). Numerous passages in this early work of Christian apologetics demonstrate that the most fashionable objections to biblical faith today are not the advanced achievement of a new and critical scientific age; contemporary criticisms of Christianity are not unprecedented and unanswerable. Rather, many of the most skeptical interpretations and arguments have already been advanced against Christian belief by such pagan philosophers in antiquity as Celsus and answered with elegant dispatch—in Celsus's case by Origen, a philosophical convert to Christianity.

But hardly anyone in America, even with an advanced academic degree, is aware that a man named Origen of Alexandria ever lived. Without any doubt, the most glaring intellectual deficiency of American higher education is an almost total neglect of the discipline of theology—and, with that, of the Age of Faith. To neglect theology is to neglect a study that absorbed the best minds of the West for more than a thousand years. Nothing else about the American university so distorts a student's understanding of the course of Western civilization. Nothing else so hinders a true appreciation of some of the greatest minds in our history. Nothing else so limits our grasp of the intellectual universe that is the object of liberal education. And nothing else so powerfully enforces the glib temporal parochialism that is the besetting vice of America's proudly cosmopolitan intellectual elite. It is impossible to do justice to our history without an acquaintance with theology, and it is impossible to understand the true limits and possibilities of human understanding.

Theology, the study of "the God of the philosophers" and of the God revealed in Scripture, is no idle exercise, nor is it a pursuit that ended with the Enlightenment. Christian theology is still studied with the utmost seriousness *today*, and not only in specialized denominational seminaries or distant monasteries, but also at Oxford and Cambridge and Tübingen and other first-class universities throughout the West. Some of the greatest minds of the twentieth century were Christian theologians, from Karl Barth to Hans Urs von Balthasar, and Americans are frankly unique among Westerners in their ignorance of this fact. As we saw, John Henry Newman's *Idea of a*

University was written to demonstrate that a university in which theology is not studied does not merit the title of "university." If you mean to acquire a genuine liberal education, you must find a way to overcome all the obstacles that the American university will put in your way. You must learn at least something of the science of theology.

❧

In the absence of a department of theology in your university, you must turn, however awkwardly, to the religion department. The academic discipline studied in such a department, however, is *not* theology. Rather, it is a variety of comparative social science that focuses on the practices of human communities deemed "religious." We saw in the previous course on the Bible that the presuppositions of the historical-critical method are such as to yield necessarily secular conclusions. The same is true for the academic study of religion more generally. Religion is here understood to be a universal human phenomenon, a set of practices differing from place to place but always serving some social function. That one religion might be true and all others false is unthinkable for the professors in the typical religion department. But the very heart of theology is the attempt to do justice to the *truth* about the God who has been revealed in the Old and New Testaments of the Bible and in the faith and practice of the churches. Theology is, in Saint Anselm's formulation, "faith seeking understanding." To start from disbelief rather than faith is no way to begin theology. But it is the best we can do in most American universities.

In almost all religion departments a course entitled something like "The Christian Tradition" can be found. Such courses can be of some value to those who have had little or no exposure to Christian practice; such courses examine the customs and beliefs of Christians as one would those of Stone Age tribes along the Amazon. To interpret Christian rituals in this anthropological way is a species of social history rather than intellectual history, and it falls far short of theology. There are, however, in many religion departments, courses with names like "Christian Thought Before 1500," and these will come closer to a general introduction to theology than any other course in the curriculum. Take this course to gain at least a glancing acquaintance with theology.

The first Christian centuries, called the Patristic Age, witnessed the intellectual explication of Christian orthodoxy by the Fathers of the Church, the bishop-theologians revered as saints who answered heresy with their decisive arguments. The work of the Fathers is distilled for us in the Nicene Creed, which is still recited by many Christian communities during

Sunday liturgy. The first Christian creed was simply "Jesus Christ is Lord." But what could that mean? What did it mean to say that Jesus of Nazareth was the Son of God, the Christ? A Christological controversy was one of the major disputed questions of those first centuries. The other main area of theological dispute involved the Trinity: Christians are monotheists who worship a God who is Father, Son, and Holy Ghost. How were Christians to understand this paradox?

In both cases, the challenge faced by the Fathers was twofold. On the one hand, they had to respond to the reductionist solutions of heretics. For example, some contended that Jesus of Nazareth was not really a man, only a spirit pretending to be a man. Others held that only God the Father is truly God, while the Son and Holy Spirit are his creatures. Such formulations ultimately fail to capture the radical claim of the Christian revelation. On the other hand, the Fathers had to avoid falling into logical contradiction that would invalidate the faith.

By the fifth century, with a series of brilliant dialectical developments by such theological giants as Athanasius, Cyril of Alexandria, Basil, Gregory of Nyssa, and Gregory of Nazianzus, the Christian Church defined its central "mysteries"—the rudiments of the faith that could not have been known by unassisted human reason but that can be shown by theology to be free of internal contradiction.

Now, the *supernatural* Christian assertions about God and the redeeming work of Jesus Christ have implications about the *nature* of man and the cosmos. True, philosophy is always the "handmaid of theology." But truer still, theology serves philosophy by enabling philosophy to reach its true end. In the first Christian centuries, the greatest theologian was also the greatest philosopher: Augustine (354-430), a bishop in Roman North Africa and author of literally hundreds of seminal works, the foremost being his *Confessions* and the *City of God*. It is often said that all of Western philosophy consists of footnotes to Plato. This is true in one sense, but it is actually more accurate to say that Western philosophy for the last fifteen hundred years has consisted of footnotes to Saint Augustine. For many of the most important questions in philosophy for more than fifteen centuries could not even have been formulated before the Christian revelation and before Augustine's grappling with the meaning of that revelation. Questions about freedom and the will and their relationship to personal identity, for example, are effectively unthinkable before Augustine; and philosophers from Descartes to Kant may best be understood as "Augustinians." The range of Augustine's interests was stupendous. Who could grapple with them all in college? But not to have read his *Confessions* is to miss perhaps the single greatest book in Western history: so singular a work is the *Confessions* that it seems nobody attempted such an autobiography of his inner life for more than a thousand years thereafter. Yet how difficult it is to find *any* course in an American university that will introduce you to this great Western mind.

❧

The fall of the western Roman Empire to invading barbarian tribes brought about the so-called Dark Ages, with classical learning kept barely alive in far-flung monasteries. The Dark Ages were neither so ignorant nor so lengthy as commonly believed, however. Boethius, executed by the Ostrogoth King Theodoric in A.D. 524, was perhaps the last representative of the uninterrupted classical Christian tradition of learning in the West. By the time of Anselm of Canterbury (1033-1109), the great flowering of the "medieval synthesis" was already at hand. Yet even in the dark depths of the ninth century, the writings of John Scotus Eriugena (810-c. 877), a monk from Ireland, demonstrate that philosophical and theological erudition and originality of the highest level were possible in the monastic schools.

Still, the second great moment for theology after the Patristic Age is the period of scholasticism in the High Middle Ages. With the Christian faith well defined and adhered to throughout Europe, Christian monks and friars in the new universities of Paris, Oxford, and elsewhere now faced a challenge from Aristotle, whose works were being translated from Arabic into Latin and thus becoming available to the Western mind for the first time in centuries. Aristotle's logical treatises, translated into Latin by Boethius, had been in constant use throughout the Dark Ages, but the newly translated works threw into doubt several of Christianity's (and of theism's) core beliefs, from the createdness of the world to the life of the soul after death.

This challenge was met most decisively in the *Summa Theologiae*, a summary of theology, by Saint Thomas Aquinas (c. 1225-1274). This huge undertaking explicates the Christian faith in the philosophical language of Aristotle and shows that nothing that reason knows as true must necessarily render Christian faith irrational. As Aquinas frequently puts it, grace (the supernatural) *perfects* nature; it does not destroy it. The *Summa* is justly famous for its style of presentation as well as for its content. By proceeding through a series of propositions, while noting objections and answering those objections in detail, Aquinas was able to display the dialectical spirit of scholastic thought. Aquinas's *Summa* thus belies the common view of the medieval mind as dogmatic or narrow. Far from it. The possibility of alternate universes, whether monogamy or polygamy is natural for man, and how it is that human beings can know anything at all are just a few of the surprising topics addressed in the *Summa*. The very first question of the *Summa* asks whether theology is necessary. The answer is yes, of course, but the objections to which Aquinas must respond are genuine ones.

Because medieval thought and theology are so little studied in American universities, few students are familiar with medieval theologians other than Aquinas. However, the essential continuity of the medieval scholastic enterprise with the theology of the Patristic Age can best be seen in the writings of Anselm of Canterbury (1033-1109) in the century before Aquinas. Moreover, while the *Summa Theologiae* is the most systematic work of its kind, on several key matters—particularly the nature of the will, both in man and in God—the theologians of Aquinas's Dominican Order were locked in unresolved dispute with the theologians of the Franciscan Order. Yet both the Dominican and Franciscan schools of theology are considered orthodox, both authentic ways by which faith can seek understanding. The first great Franciscan theologian was Saint Bonaventure (c. 1217-1274), a contemporary of Aquinas. And in the two generations after Aquinas, the Franciscans Duns Scotus (c. 1266-1308) and William of Ockham (c. 1285-1349) raised what might be called Augustinian objections against Aquinas's Aristotelianism.

The views of Scotus and Ockham, in turn, are generally understood to have prepared the way for the Protestant Reformation of the sixteenth century. Martin Luther (1483-1546) was a great Ockhamite Augustinian, and John Calvin (1509-1564) is probably best understood as a brilliant late medieval scholastic theologian attempting to read Augustine anew. One result of the Reformation theology was that the traditional Christian marriage of theology and philosophy was annulled. In the churches of the Reformation, theology thereafter proceeds almost exclusively by way of scriptural commentary.

Perhaps the most pernicious development in the teaching of this material in recent years is the tendency of professors to champion the views of heretics against the orthodox theologians. Certain professors have "rediscovered" the Gnostic gospels and the writings of Arius, Pelagius, and Nestorius and have found these teachings more congenial to the modern mind. They like to suggest that what is considered orthodox Christianity is purely the result of arbitrary exercises of power by the hierarchical and patriarchal Church. In taking this deconstructive view, they profoundly skew a true understanding of the theology of the first centuries. For in fact, on several occasions the orthodox position was a distinctly minority view that won the assent of the faithful primarily by the force of greater logical coherence. To study the controversy between the heretics and the champions of orthodoxy can be useful, however, for in this way you can more readily see how dogmatic theology proceeds "negatively."

There are numerous secondary works that will help you to understand the orthodox theological tradition in a way that does not succumb to trite deconstruction. G. L. Prestige's *God in Patristic Thought* (London, 1936; reprinted, 1956) is an exhaustive study, though sometimes quite technical. J. N. D. Kelly's *Early Christian Doctrines* (London, 1958; fifth edition, 1985) is a balanced and readable account of a range of disputed Patristic questions. Leo Donald Davis, S.J., *The First Seven Ecumenical Councils (325-787): Their History and Theology* (Wilmington, Del., 1987) is also valuable. Jaroslav Pelikan's monumental *The Christian Tradition: A History of the Development of Doctrine* (Chicago, 1971-1989) is an encyclopedic source of information about the formal teaching of the Church. It is particularly good in its account of individual thinkers.

John Henry Newman's *Essay on the Development of Christian Doctrine* (London, 1845; sixth edition, 1989) is one of the greatest theological treatments of the idea of theological tradition written in any language. It is as much a primary work in the thought of the nineteenth century as it is a work to aid understanding of historical developments. Newman's earlier work, *The Arians of the Fourth Century* (London, 1833; third edition, 1919) is a still-useful model of Patristic scholarship that opens up the heart of the disputed question of those early days.

Vernon Bourke's *Augustine's Love of Wisdom* (West Lafayette, Ind., 1992) is an excellent philosophical biography, while Peter Brown's *Augustine of Hippo* (Berkeley, 1967) represents the findings of the latest scholarship.

It is more difficult to find satisfactory secondary works on medieval theology; the philosophy of that age has been more studied. Josef Pieper's *Scholasticism: Personalities and Problems of Medieval Philosophy*, translated by Richard and Clara Winston (New York, 1960), is the place to begin, and Frederick Copleston's *A History of Medieval Philosophy* (New York, 1972) is a standard reference. Etienne Gilson treats medieval theology and philosophy with the highest seriousness in *The Spirit of Mediaeval Philosophy* translated by A.H.C. Downes (London, 1936), *The Christian Philosophy of St. Thomas Aquinas* translated by G. A. Elrington (St. Louis, 1937), and *The Philosophy of St. Bonaventure* translated by Illtyd Trethowan (London, 1938). Gilson in turn recommended to students G. K. Chesterton's biography *Saint Thomas Aquinas* (London, 1933; reissued 1974), saying that it captured the spirit of Aquinas's project better than any other book available.

In addition, Aidan Nichols, *The Shape of Catholic Theology* (Edinburgh, 1991), offers a view of the contemporary course of the discipline of theology.

MODERN POLITICAL THEORY

HALF A CENTURY AGO, the political writings of Luther and Calvin would have been prominent on the syllabus of any American college course in modern political thought. Today, that course begins with Machiavelli (1469-1527) and excludes any consideration of the Reformers—or, indeed, of such Catholic thinkers of the sixteenth century as Thomas More (1478-1535) or Robert Bellarmine (1542-1621). In so presenting the history of political philosophy, the contemporary course indicates that its primary concern will be the problem of *modernity*—*die Neuzeit* or "new time," as it is called in German—which is, among other things, an age characterized by a growing secularism. One of the advantages of the current order of presentation is that it enables us to see more clearly how *being modern* might constitute a problem. One of the disadvantages of excluding Christian political theologies is that the dialectical dependence of modernity on Christianity is thereby obscured.

At the beginning of his longest work, the *Discourses on the First Ten Books of Livy*, Machiavelli implicitly compares himself with that icon of the new man, Christopher Columbus. Machiavelli writes that he has set out to discover new continents in the moral and political world: this, in a book that is, on the surface, a commentary on an ancient Roman work of history. In addition, Machiavelli wrote *The Prince,* a handbook for ruthless statecraft in the turbulent world of Renaissance Italy. To be sure, the Renaissance was a rebirth of classical (pre-Christian) learning, but it was also something *new.* Machiavelli's "new modes and orders" were to be instituted *against* Christianity in a way that pagan philosophy and practice never had been. Consequently, to investigate the course of modern political theory is to approach a question of the first importance that nevertheless seldom is considered: What is *modern man*?

❧

Aristotle held that political science (or political philosophy) was the architectonic inquiry. Since it is the business of statecraft to oversee all human initiatives and to assign each person to his place, it is therefore the business of political philosophy, after examining all human interests in due order, to provide the overarching pattern into which those activities will be fitted. For Aristotle, the *polis* (the "city") comes into being because of human necessity, but its aim is the good life. According to Greek political philosophy, then, life in the *polis* is the natural *end* for man. But Christianity introduced an unprecedented political and philosophical problem, for Jesus had said, "My Kingdom is not of this world." Life in the city is *not* man's ultimate goal: salvation is, and salvation is personal. Christianity thereby "loosened" the ties that bound men together in their particular political orders.

But unlike either Judaism or Islam, Christianity did not present itself as a divine rule that superintends all the details of life. Had this been the case, political life as the Greeks understood it would simply have been reconstituted at the level of the believing community. In both Judaism and Islam, the political and religious spheres coincide exactly and do so on religion's terms. But for Christianity the secular realm is, in principle, free to organize itself independently. Jesus had also said, "Render unto Caesar the things that are Caesar's," thus bestowing a certain autonomy on secular affairs. Still, the Church's divine mission is to lead all men to salvation. Having renounced secular governance, the Church must nonetheless claim the right to regulate anything that might put salvation in peril. In the Christian dispensation, the secular realm is never, finally, free. An irresolvable conflict between *sacerdotium* and *imperium*, between pope and emperor, seems essential to Christianity. Some twentieth-century commentators, such as Christopher Dawson, have seen this very tension as the driving force of true progress in the West. But the modern political philosophers did not see it this way. Instead, it is just this conflict that they set out to resolve decisively. In the process, modern political philosophy brought into being *modern man.*

Thus, we may speak of a "modern project." For the modern political philosophers did not merely seek to capture the truth about man's place in the cosmos and in society; they also set out to transform the human world. In doing so, modern political philosophy diverges systematically from both ancient and medieval thought. In reaction to both Christian and classical political thought, the moderns begin by "lowering the sights" of political communities. Modern thinkers in various ways insist that the end for man in politics is not the good life but mere life, comfortable security. This end in turn is accomplished, perhaps paradoxically, by the liberation of human passions. Whereas all ancient and medieval political philosophy sought to temper human passions through an education into virtue, understood as a kind of voluntary self-constraint, modern political philosophy seeks to understand and foster *freedom.*

❧

Human freedom is of course nothing new. But pursuing

freedom as an end, and not merely for the few but for all men equally—that is a radical novelty. For Plato and Aristotle both, freedom was thought neither to be the natural state of man nor to be an unqualified good. After all, it seems obvious that most men, when left free, will seek to satisfy their vulgar desires rather than pursue any higher and specifically human ends. Freedom can only be good for you if you can use your freedom well. Thus, for the ancients *virtue,* not freedom, is the proper pursuit of political men. Any purported natural "right" to liberty would depend upon virtue. Virtue comes *first* in ancient political thought, and it is a public rather than a private concern.

But for the moderns, freedom comes first. And this contention precipitates a "transvaluation of values" beyond the realm of politics. The most obvious example of this concerns the relative valuing of political life and family life. The ancients associated politics with the good life or human flourishing. Political participation was thought intrinsically valuable, an end in itself. In contrast, the family or household (the *oikos,* in Greek) was understood as the realm of slavish "economics," where the mere necessities of life were secured. For modern men, however, something of the reverse is true. We tend to consider politics to be a matter of technical economic division and boundary-setting. Political life is nothing very exalted, more a distraction from "what really matters." Conversely, we hold family life to be the privileged sphere of human fulfillment. Only a modern man would say that the end of all human striving is to be happy at home. Such is the power of political philosophy.

After Machiavelli, the modern pursuit of freedom proceeds by proposing a rival to the biblical Eden—the "state of nature"—from which men emerge not by divine expulsion but by choice, by agreement, by *contract*. In the accounts of Hobbes (1588-1679), Locke (1632-1704), and Rousseau (1712-1778)—each quite distinct in his theorizing—the justice that men construct for themselves is based not on conformity with nature but on reason's cunning overcoming of nature's inconvenience. Talk of the "state of nature" with its "natural rights" secured in civil society by a "social contract" strikes us as a moderate commonplace, but these are frankly revolutionary concepts. David Hume (1711-1776) was the political philosopher in our tradition who called attention to the extremism in these views—*our* views. In the subsequent thought of German philosophers—from Kant (1724-1804) through Hegel (1770-1831) and Marx (1818-1883) to Nietzsche (1844-1900)—the philosophical burden of human freedom grew acute. For human freedom to be truly free, it must be utterly free of the restrictions of nature and tradition. For men to be truly free, these Germans say, each in his own way, men must be, or become, *gods*.

Practically speaking, you must make sure the course you take is in *modern* political theory and not *contemporary* political theory. The modern period begins in the sixteenth century, and some would say that modernity has already come to an end, having been succeeded by a postmodern age. Whatever the case, the work of such contemporary academic political thinkers as John Rawls or Richard Rorty or Jürgen Habermas is of only narrow interest. None is a central figure in the Western tradition.

Frequently the course in modern political theory is well taught, but two pedagogic approaches can misdirect your attention away from the really important questions you must grapple with. On the one hand, there are professors who will so focus their reading of the philosophical texts on the "contexts" of their times that there will be nothing we could possibly learn from them about how to order our life together today. In this case, modern political theory becomes merely a matter of antiquarian interest. On the other hand, there are professors who will spend much of their classroom time judging these great thinkers for their failure to live up to *our* standards of justice and right, particularly their bad record with regard to women and minorities. In this case, modern political theory becomes an exercise in flattering the prejudices of the present age.

The study of political philosophy is most valuable when you make use of the thought of the various philosophers to challenge your own unexamined opinions. Rather than recoiling at Machiavelli's amorality or Hobbes's totalitarianism or Kant's absolutism, ask yourself how these philosophers would react to *your* opinions. Would they find them wanting? Ask yourself what it is about the human world and the nature of man that these thinkers *see* and that you do not see as clearly, or at all. And because our American prejudices reflect the thought of John Locke and John Stuart Mill (1806-1873), you must make an extra effort to be critical when examining those two thinkers.

The readings in this course are difficult and lengthy. Indeed, students often find this course the hardest of the eight courses in this core curriculum. Fortunately, sound secondary literature in political philosophy is widely available. For a straightforward account of what each of the thinkers is actually saying (not always apparent on a first reading), try Dante Germino's *Machiavelli to Marx* (Chicago, 1972; reprinted, 1979). Pierre Manent's *Intellectual History of Liberalism,* translated by Rebecca Balinski (Princeton, N.J., 1994), is especially telling concerning the anti-Christian orientation of modern political theory. Charles N. R. McCoy's *The Structure of Political Thought* (New York, 1963) is the effort of a Thomist to understand the meaning of modernity in light of the permanent structure of human nature. Eric Voegelin's *From Enlightenment to Revolution* (Durham, N.C., 1975) examines several less prominent political theorists to illuminate the trajectory of modernity.

For particular modern political thinkers, the essays in Strauss & Cropsey's *History of Political Philosophy* (Chicago, 1963; third edition, 1987) are usually excellent.

SHAKESPEARE

In Shakespeare's *Henry VI: Part III*, the magnificently wicked Duke of Gloucester (later Richard III) compares his villainy to the precepts of "the murderous Machiavel"—that is, to Machiavelli, the philosopher we found at the dawn of the modern age. *Julius Caesar* is one of a number of Shakespeare's plays set in antiquity, and the bard populates *A Midsummer Night's Dream* with minor pagan deities. *The Merchant of Venice* is Shakespeare's meditation on the relationship between the revealed Law of the Old Testament and the Law of Grace instituted by the New Covenant in Christ. Shakespeare (1564-1616), in short, is the poet who stands uniquely at the intersection of modern man, ancient man, and Christian man. He also notoriously engages in anachronism, refers to such impossible locales as the "shores of Bohemia," and often indiscriminately mixes pagan and Christian references in the same play. But far from constituting the forgivable "mistakes" of a precritical and uneducated mind, Shakespeare in this way signals his theme: the representation of human nature as such, in all its diversity and its unity.

It is a commonplace to say that Shakespeare's position for us in the English-speaking world is like that of Homer for the Greeks, Virgil for the Romans, Dante for the Italians, or Cervantes for the Spaniards. But this may actually understate Shakespeare's genius; he may simply be more universal even than those who are ranked among his peers. Shakespeare holds the poetic mirror of his imagination up to all of nature and to all of history. He invites us to delight and marvel at what he discovers. And we do. One excellent reason for taking a course on the plays of Shakespeare is the sheer *joy* of it.

We saw that in Plato's *Republic*, Socrates argues for the absolute superiority of philosophy to poetry. He even speaks of an "old quarrel" between the two, noting that since the poets sometimes portray the prospering of the wicked and the misfortunes of the just, the poets are a threat to virtue. Shifting his ground from morals to aesthetics, Socrates adduces as key evidence for philosophy's superiority the fact that there is no poet among the Greeks who can write both tragedy and comedy well. What the poets relate is striking but one-sided and therefore distorted. Life is *both* tragic and comic, and yet perhaps neither ultimately tragic nor comic. Philosophers, on the contrary, transcend poetic partiality to approach the *whole*. This Socratic observation about poetic limitation proved true for centuries. But among Shakespeare's plays may be counted some of the most profound tragedies and most delightful comedies in all literature. If any poet can challenge Plato's claim about philosophy's supremacy, it is Shakespeare. His vision extends to the whole of man's wide world, while capturing the innermost workings of the human heart.

❧

By convention we divide Shakespeare's plays into three kinds: tragedies, comedies, and histories. Among the histories, however, there are tragic endings (general woe and death for Richard II), and there are comic endings (Henry V's wooing of the French princess following victory at Agincourt). In Shakespeare, life and art thus mingle. He in effect reveals that the stories of "real life," the life of each historical human being, can hold as much meaning as the most powerful mythic tale. Each human life holds a fascination beyond any archetype. Shakespeare marvels lovingly at humanity, and we in turn share in that wonder.

Here among the striking facts of Shakespeare's work is that he did not invent his plots. Rather, he took well-known historical episodes or popular tales lying ready to hand and retold what was familiar to his audiences. Where, then, is Shakespeare's creativity—if, indeed, creativity is the measure by which to judge a poet? In his incomparable language of course. But beyond that, Shakespeare's genius is expressed primarily in his characterizations. Our deepest interest is drawn by Shakespeare's characters—about 900 of them throughout the plays, and yet each an irreducible individual, each with a life of his own. Falstaff alone is a miracle.

A comparison of MacBeth and Richard III illustrates Shakespeare's unmatched ability to portray the details of our humanity. Both MacBeth and Richard III are soldiers, both usurpers who obtain the throne through treason, both driven by ambition. In both cases, their futures are foretold by supernatural signs and they both lose their thrones in battle with the legitimate heir. Yet where MacBeth is "too full of the milk of human kindness," Richard III is remorselessly evil. MacBeth's ambition is a matter of vanity, revolving around honor; whereas Richard's ambition is oriented to power and driven by pride. MacBeth is soft where Richard is strong. On the surface, their stories are the same, but how different are these two men—or rather, these two fictions who seem so alive in Shakespeare's verse. As Shakespeare's wisest reader, Samuel Johnson, aptly commented, "[H]e that has read Shakespeare with attention will perhaps find little new in the crowded world."

❧

Some students object to studying Shakespeare in college because he is so familiar to them from high school. They therefore associate him with a discarded intellectual naiveté, judging themselves "beyond" the bard. Of course this is not true, for Shakespeare is always ahead of us. Harold Bloom goes so far (too far) as to suggest that Shakespeare has "invented" us, for much of what we recognize in human nature has been observed *for* us by Shakespeare. So well has he represented nature that now we may well judge nature by *his* artistic standards. Now that we have begun to grasp the sweep of the Western tradition, however, other questions can also emerge for us. For example, we must now inevitably ask, How do Shakespeare's tragedies compare to those of the Greeks? How do his comedies compare? What can the differences and similarities tell us about the human condition?

Hegel observed that in ancient tragedy, conflict erupts *between* antagonists, such as Creon and Antigone, each representing a principle of action. In the prototypical modern tragedy, *Hamlet*, however, conflict rages *within* the protagonist. There is greater depth to the human soul in Shakespeare's tragedies, and Hegel believed this to be a legacy of Christianity. It is certainly the case that Shakespeare's tragedies appear more horrifying to us than the works of Sophocles. What accounts for this effect? And what does this effect mean for Shakespeare's vision of the world? Is the greater *depth* of Shakespearean tragedy brought about because of the greater *heights* opened up for the human soul by Christian hope?

For often very bad reasons, we tend to consider tragedy a more profound, a more important genre than comedy. This may be one reason we tend to underestimate the mind of the Middle Ages. For medieval men did not write tragedies. When Chaucer attempted one, he set it in the ancient world and used the story to illustrate the difference Christian grace makes. The world is tragic without grace, but since grace has come, it is tragic no longer. The greatest achievement of the medieval mind could only have been a divine *comedy* (Dante). Tragedy returns to the world with the Renaissance, and Shakespeare is a great tragic writer. But Shakespeare is also a writer of *profound* comedies. His comedies, however, are utterly unlike those of the ancients. For in Shakespeare, human love is not simply ridiculous. While love perhaps begins as something low, and while it may lead us astray, it also may be made sublime. His comedies always end with marriage, the hallowed fulfillment of human love. Shakespeare can teach us how to love.

If the poet were to respond to the philosopher's claimed supremacy, he would note that human nature is such that poetic representation can stir the moral imagination beyond the deepest philosophy. We may learn in Aristotle's *Ethics* about the virtue of courage, and Aristotle may even convince us—intellectually—that we must become virtuous. But Henry V's Saint Crispin's Day speech *moves* us. We then *know* courage better. We may anatomize human loves with impressive philosophical skill, but everyone knows that love can only be understood from the inside. In our concreteness, somehow artistic representation provides an icon of actual experience, always the best of teachers. And in the end, Shakespeare knows quite well what he thinks about the limitations of the philosophers. In *The Tempest,* he presents for our consideration the philosopher Prospero, whose philosophical island idyll is seen as ultimately irresponsible. Does Plato really comprehend the poet better than Shakespeare comprehends the philosopher?

❧

Shakespeare has largely retained his privileged place in the curricula of many university English departments. However, precisely because Shakespeare is the very epitome of a classic or a canonical figure, he seems always the favorite target of the latest vogue in critical theory. Thus, you must beware the theoretical lens through which Shakespeare may be taught to you.

Today, deconstruction has become passé, but it has often merely metamorphosed into a critical school known as "new historicism" or "cultural materialism." For critics of this persuasion, inheritors of Karl Marx, literary texts are cultural artifacts reflecting the power structure of their authors' societies. Like any other author, Shakespeare's works are interrogated to "show" how the bard is merely mouthing the ideology of his day. Shakespeare is an early modern bourgeois. The objections to such an approach are legion, the foremost being that in trapping the poet in his context, there is nothing one could possibly learn from him. There is thus little point in reading him. And of course, if all writers are merely reflections of power relations, isn't that also true of these contemporary academic writers of criticism? Why read them?

Shakespeare's plays have also proven fertile ground recently for the ruminations of feminists and theorists of sex and gender. Some feminists denounce him as a patriarch, but more recently there is an enthusiasm for Shakespeare's alleged ambiguity about sex and gender: so often comic plot developments involve cross-dressing, and of course, in Shakespeare's time, all the women's roles would have been played by boys. But while some of these critics are very intelligent, they push their arguments to farcical extremes. Perhaps the best response to those who claim to discover themes of "sex and gender" in Shakespeare is to respond that he is much more clearly a poet concerned with "love and marriage."

To learn more about Shakespeare and his times, you may consult Andrew Gurr's *William Shakespeare: The Extraordinary*

Life of the Most Successful Writer of All Time (1996). Eric Sams' *The Real Shakespeare: Retrieving the Early Years, 1564-1594* (New Haven, Conn., 1995) sheds new light on the bard's formative influences.

C. S. Lewis's *Discarded Image* (Cambridge, 1964; reprinted, 1994) is a brilliant and brilliantly crafted account of the late medieval and early modern worldview that formed the background understanding of Shakespeare's audience.

C. L. Barber's *Shakespeare's Festive Comedy* (Princeton, N.J., 1959; Cleveland, 1966) is a classic work exploring the Christian elements of the bard's comedies. R. Chris Hassel's *Faith and Folly in Shakespeare's Romantic Comedies* (Athens, Ga., 1980) is a more contemporary work in the same spirit.

A. C. Bradley's *Shakespearean Tragedy* (New York, 1905; third edition, 1992) studies the heroes of the tragedies, appreciating their depth and differentiating their plights from the crises found in ancient tragedy. Roy Battenhouse's *Shakespearean Tragedy: Its Art and Christian Premises* (Bloomington, Ind., 1969) argues that the peculiarities of Shakespearean tragedy are a result of the explicitly Christian dimension of Shakespeare's mind.

Robert Ornstein, *A Kingdom for a Stage: The Achievement of Shakespeare's History Plays* (Cambridge, Mass., 1972) is the best general introduction to the history plays, arguing that they contain a political teaching.

For an accessible response to contemporary schools of criticism, see Brian Vickers's *Returning to Shakespeare* (London, 1989). A more sophisticated defense of traditional interpretations of Shakespeare may be found in Anthony David Nuttall, *A New Mimesis: Shakespeare and the Representation of Reality* (London, 1983). The first third of Nuttall's volume constitutes a sophisticated expression of the old argument that art is valuable in its representative function. The remainder of the book is a delightful contemporary reading of Shakespeare freed from the shackles of ideology.

For another perspective, G. Wilson Knight's *Wheel of Fire* (London, 1930; fourth edition, 1977) is a stunning example of the critical insights that can be gained when attention is paid to the imagery embedded in Shakespeare's poetic language.

U. S. HISTORY BEFORE 1865

MACHIAVELLI'S AIM was to institute "new modes and orders" in the moral world, and Shakespeare set his play *The Tempest* on Caliban's mysterious island home across the sea. In both cases these men were reflecting on an historical fact that looms enormous in the history of the West: the discovery of the New World. While ideas certainly have consequences, the facts of historical experience shape no less profoundly the human imagination, and so with the experience of the Discovery.

Columbus had set sail to find a trade route to China, an advanced civilization whose political upheavals had already affected the economy of the Roman Empire in the days of the Caesars. But Columbus encountered something more remarkable than Cathay—an entire continent seemingly in a state of nature and thus, to the European mind, the property of no one. Never before had Western men experienced anything remotely like this. Perhaps no one in history had. The *idea* of America seized the European mind and remains part of all Americans' identity. That idea is of an unconquered but conquerable wilderness where one may escape and start anew in freedom and independence. Peasants leaving the land for the medieval towns had experienced a kind of liberation, but the New World promised something more startling, an opportunity to reform the human situation for all, to overcome at last the weight of the past in the name of freedom and nature.

However much philosophers and humanists had speculated about utopia in previous centuries, utopia had always been "nowhere," situated in the shadowy mental realm of myth or fantasy. Now, a seemingly utopian territory had been discovered that was incontestably *real.* Time and again America has been the home of utopian projects, from the Puritans' Godly Experiment, to Oneida in upstate New York, to David Koresh's apocalyptic commune in Waco. But above these smaller experiments, many of them motivated by religious enthusiasm, there is the overarching political project of the United States itself, the American Experiment of an Empire of Liberty fulfilling its Manifest Destiny as "the last best hope of men on earth." Surely there are utopian (and messianic) elements evident even in our Constitutional prudence. And this peculiarity—an extremism embedded in our moderation—is what you will explore in a course on the first "half" of American history.

The United States is a nation with a known origin, a *founding*. Our history as a people does not in the first instance run off into an immemorial past, nor do our political practices descend to us from before the dawn of recorded history. America's political forms are the result of a choice. Moreover, that choice was not arbitrary but was guided by principles believed to reflect the moral realities of human life. Whether these principles arose from reason or experience remains a disputed question.

The two questions that naturally face Americans when considering our history are these: (1) Are America's founding principles sound or unsound? and (2) Has America "turned out" as the founders intended (i.e., have America's political principles worked)?

These questions assume that we already know what America's founding principles are; as we shall see, however, such a belief is not really warranted.

These questions have been answered quite differently at different points in our history. Charles Beard, writing in the 1930s in the midst of capitalism's apparent collapse, discerned at work in the U. S. Constitution the unjust self-interest of an early class of powerful possessive individualists. For Beard, America was ill founded, but America had indeed turned out as intended, only to face the "inherent contradictions" of capitalism in the Great Depression.

Today, however, the typical answer to these questions is that America's founding principles were sound but were originally incompletely applied (the equal rights of slaves and women were not secured by the original Constitution). This incompletion may be attributed to the founders' inability to see beyond their historical context, or to a conscious and malign intent on the founders' part, or to their conscious calculation and hope of setting in motion a process leading to "liberty and justice for all." Whatever the case, insofar as America has turned out "badly," it is said to be because of those incomplete applications of the founding principles. In this account of our history, America's core principle is a commitment to equal freedom. The expansion of "rights" is thus America's most important story. Such, for example, is the implication of Eric Foner's widely assigned but dubious book, *Reconstruction: America's Unfinished Revolution* (New York, 1988). Such is the promise said to be held by "our living Constitution." Such also, in a slightly different register, is the view of a prominent group of contemporary neoconservative political thinkers.

The narrative of expanding liberty is indeed majestic, and there is much truth to it. But it also neglects much in

America's history and therefore obscures full understanding. Above all, this interpretation of America requires us to believe that nothing has been lost in the unfolding of American history except injustice, to lose which, of course, is no loss at all. But in fact, genuine human goods have sometimes waned as our rights and freedoms have waxed. America's progress has a *tragic* dimension as well.

To interpret American history through the lens of a rights-based individualism is to say that America is the historical actualization of the liberal tradition in political theory, a tradition most closely associated with Locke. Louis Hartz's famous book *The Liberal Tradition in America* (New York, 1955; San Diego, Calif., 1991) argued for a Lockean consensus in American history. Because America was a nation "born equal," Hartz claimed that Americans were exclusively devoted to one form or another of bourgeois liberalism; both radical socialism and European-style conservatism were instinctively believed to be un-American. Again, there is some truth in this, but one immediate problem for Hartz's thesis was that he had to write the South and the Civil War *out* of American history.

Two further responses to the liberal thesis have emerged in recent years. One group of scholars argues that early America's authentic political tradition is really civic republicanism, a term that designates strong democracy and political participation of the sort that characterized the ancient

Greek *polis*. Samuel Adams spoke of his desire to see America as a "Christian Sparta." For the civic republican interpreters, America's founding aspiration was not the "right to be left alone," but rather the right to participate in decisions affecting the individual and the community. Rights are then a *secondary* concern to democracy.

But Adams spoke of a *Christian* Sparta. The other major interpretive school of recent years has explored the decisive role played by Christianity throughout American history. Both liberalism and civic republicanism have a secular orientation, but many of their themes have correlates in American Christianity's faith and practice. Liberalism speaks of individual freedom, and Christian conversion promises a truth that will set men free. Civic republicanism speaks of self-governing communities, and Congregationalist Christianity is concretely organized in just such a fashion. The religious beliefs of such early national figures as Madison, Jefferson, and Adams are a matter of dispute. But the religious enthusiasm of the ratifying publics of the original states is not, and this fact must be remembered when we seek to discover the original understanding of the American Constitution.

❧

Today, American History is among the most politicized of the disciplines. Fashionable historians vacillate between, on the one hand, denouncing America for its exclusion or marginalization of women, minorities, and the poor from the promise of American life, and, on the other, championing the unsung (and sometimes simply mythical) contributions made by women, minorities, and the poor to the development of American life. But all historians seem united in holding America to be an "exceptional" country, the embodiment of an *idea*. The challenge for an American hoping to develop a genuine historical imagination is to see America as a *not* wholly exceptional country—to note, for example, that the unstable countries of Latin America for the most part adopted variants of the American Constitution, while stable Canada was founded in explicit repudiation of American principles. Such recognitions are where *thought* begins.

The most powerful sustained argument for the classical republican thesis concerning the American founding is Bernard Bailyn's *Ideological Origins of the American Revolution* (Cambridge, Mass., 1967; enlarged edition, 1992). Barry Shain's *Myth of American Individualism* (Princeton, N.J., 1994) in turn provides the evidence and assesses the theoretical importance of exclusivist Reformed Protestant communalism.

Harry Jaffa's *Crisis of the House Divided* (Garden City, N.Y., 1959; Chicago, 1999) is a philosophical reading of the Lincoln-Douglas debates that interprets American experience through the lens of classical natural right. Jaffa sees Lincoln as "completing" the founding. For a powerful rejoinder to Jaffa that champions a strongly states'-rights understanding of America's original compact, see M. E. Bradford, *Original Intentions: On the Making and Ratification of the United States Constitution* (Athens, Ga., 1993).

Willmoore Kendall and George Carey's *Basic Symbols of the American Political Tradition* (Baton Rouge, La., 1970; Washington, D.C., 1995) examines a series of American founding documents of the late eighteenth century in the light of previous American founding moments. Kendall and Carey discern an American tradition of a self-governing "virtuous people."

Herbert Storing's *What the Anti-Federalists Were For* (Chicago, 1981) is a brilliant recovery of the views of America's early losing side. A commonplace observation among political theorists is that America now possesses Federalist institutions operating in an anti-Federalist fashion.

The great Southern alternative understanding of the America experiment requires careful study if we are to avoid shallow ideological interpretations of our history. Eugene Genovese's *Roll, Jordan, Roll* (New York, 1974; reprinted 1976) is the best book on slavery in America; and his book *The Slaveholders' Dilemma* (Columbia, S.C., 1992) is a sympathetic account of the way in which the ruling classes in the antebellum South viewed their world. Two books that present

Southern views in a striking fashion and that serve to balance the likes of Eric Foner are E. Merton Coulter's *The South During Reconstruction, 1865-1877* (Baton Rouge, La., 1947) and Ludwell Johnson's *Division and Reunion: America 1848-1877* (New York, 1978).

For a work arguing for continuity between America and the European past, see Russell Kirk's *Roots of American Order* (Malibu, Calif., 1981; Washington, D.C., 1991). Gary L. Gregg's *Vital Remnants: America's Founding and the Western Tradition* (Wilmington, Del., ISI Books, 1999) collects several notable essays exploring the same theme.

NINETEENTH-CENTURY EUROPEAN INTELLECTUAL HISTORY

BY ABOUT THE END of their second year in college, American students have acquired an assortment of concepts and ideas by which they are able to interpret their world, and they are impressed with themselves because of the intellectual *power* such mediating schema provide. They may be familiar with the Hawthorne Experiment and understand the Oedipal Complex. They may say knowing things about *gemeinschaft* and *gesellschaft* and about alienation. They may analyze their friends' behaviors as the manifestation of sublimated desires. They may speak with assurance about the social construction of reality and object to a friend's generalization as relying on evidence which is only "anecdotal."

That an individual's thinking proceeds by means of mediating concepts—mental "lenses," if you will—is no surprise. Such mediating concepts may be found in many forms: in scriptural exemplars or in historical knowledge or in literary precedent, for example. What *is* striking about the (very)

American minds of American undergraduates is that their common stock of mediating concepts is drawn *overwhelmingly* from the social sciences, which the Europeans call more aptly the "sciences of man" or the "human sciences," those academic disciplines born in the nineteenth century. The American mind of today has thus in large part been constituted by European ideas of very recent and very particular provenance. To study the intellectual history of the nineteenth century provides you with the chance to polish your conceptual lenses for even deeper insight, and also to discover, perhaps, that what you took to be a powerfully useful lens is in fact a *blinder*.

❧

The great synthetic mind who stands at the dawn of the nineteenth century is the German philosopher Hegel (1770-1831). Into him flow both the rationalism of the Enlightenment and the insights of the Romantic reaction to the excesses of Enlightenment. For the next century, much Western thought might be understood as a prolonged response to Hegel, and that response is disproportionately undertaken in the German language. In many ways, the nineteenth century was the German century. Even America came under Germany's cultural sway as the institutional Germanization of the American university in the first quarter of the twentieth century led to the Germanization of the American mind.

Hegel is the great nineteenth-century thinker, and therefore the prototypically *modern* thinker, for at least three reasons.

First, Hegel's philosophical system is not just a series of discrete ideas but the elaboration of one Big Idea. The coming to self-consciousness of *Geist* or Spirit in history is the grandest of grand narratives; Hegel's system endeavors to be a Theory of Everything, from the meaning of music to religion to culture to economics. And the modern Western mind has been strongly attracted to such ingenious comprehensive theories resting on the most parsimonious of foundations. We find such theories *impressive*. We accord *respect* to a thinker who can concoct one, but the grounds for our doing so is by no means clear. The idea of the grand narrative is also the point on which turns the contemporary postmodern assault on modern thought. For the postmoderns, grand narrative is now passé. Or is it truer to say that the supersession of all grand narratives *is* the postmodern grand narrative?

Second, Hegel's attempt to understand history philosophically is an example of the secularization of the Western mind. In old-fashioned accounts of nineteenth-century intellectual history, historians would speak of the "coming of age" of modern man, the mind's final liberation from clerical supervision and medieval superstition. The story of the nineteenth century is of course more complex than that. In fact, Christianity was terribly weak throughout the eighteenth century and experienced a robust popular, doctrinal, and institutional revival in the nineteenth century. At the same time, however, it is true that during the nineteenth century the human sciences co-opted Christian categories and concepts. Purporting to uncover the rational truths behind Christian "myths," the practitioners of the human sciences emptied Christian ideas of their content and kept the shells. Hegel's particular appropriation was the doctrine of Providence, and his innovation would have lasting impact on Western thought.

The Renaissance understood itself as a rebirth of classical culture—that is to say, a turning back to the past rather than something new. However, the discoveries of that age soon precipitated the Battle of the Books, a debate about the relative importance of the revived ancient and new modern learning. Nineteenth century men had no such debate. They simply *knew* that modern times were better. They knew this because thinkers like Hegel had devised arguments for the *necessity* of historical progress. In understanding the philosophical or scientific "laws" of history in the manner of Hegel or his successors, one could claim to understand the mind of God better than any priest or bishop.

Third, Hegel's claimed insight into the structure of history meant that he was relieved (as were his epigones, such as Marx and many of us today) of the obligation to argue for the justice or goodness of his preferred social arrangements. Whether we liked it or not, Hegel said, history was heading in a certain direction, and nothing could stop it, much less reverse it. In a time of disputed values, such an argument was an apparent trump. Hegel purported to demonstrate something *objective*, a fact, rather than to argue pointlessly over something *subjective*, values. This dubious intellectual shorthand—claiming to be on the side of the "inevitable" future—remains deeply engrained in us today. But Hegel's understanding of history is also paradigmatic of the modern sciences of man in another way: in its virtual elimination of human agency. Men are no longer understood as free and responsible *causes;* rather, they are understood as *effects* of forces beyond their control. Humanity's coming of age seems to entail for the modern mind a considerable deflation of humanity.

By consensus, the other major figures of modern, or nineteenth-century, intellectual history are Darwin (1809-1882), Marx (1818-1883), Nietzsche (1844-1900), and Freud (1856-1939). These four are the paradigmatic figures of their age and ours. Like Hegel, they are intellectual system builders, founders of entirely new academic disciplines, human sciences based on a single insight. All of these thinkers are secularizers. They find they can no longer believe in the biblical religion. Yet try as some may, they cannot simply return to a pre-Christian understanding of nature. And so their naturalism is peculiarly post-Christian. And their humanism has in each case a peculiarly inhuman quality, for in each case man is reduced to an epiphenomenon of other influences, and largely materialist influences at that. Can such as these truly represent the "highest" intellectual achievements of the Western tradition? Or are we not driven, rather, to reconsider precisely that view of historical progress which is so striking a legacy of modern times?

❧

In history departments, the course covering the key thinkers mentioned above might be called something like "Makers of the Modern Mind" or "Western Mind in Crisis." Or you may be able to find only a course in, for example, "European Intellectual History after 1815," which will combine the nineteenth and twentieth centuries. But the twentieth century is less significant intellectually. Beyond some genuine advances in the natural sciences, very few of the currents of twentieth-century thought are original. Communism, nationalism, social democracy, Christian democracy, Darwinism, feminism, neo-paganism, racism, behaviorism, and utilitarianism are just a few twentieth-century movements with roots in the nineteenth century. Focus your attention there.

You may encounter two distinct teaching problems in a modern intellectual history course. First, your professor may provide an excessively narrow interpretation of the modern world, a "big theory" which is inevitably distorting. Perhaps the modern age is thought to be the age of progress, and so progressive texts will be supplied, with each successive radicalization following as if of necessity from the previous. Or perhaps the modern mind is thought to represent the fulfillment of the Enlightenment project, in which case secularism is stressed. Keep in mind that to characterize an age in such a sweeping way is to follow in the footsteps of Hegel. Try to be more critical, while also acknowledging the partial truth in virtually every Big Idea.

Second, the discipline of intellectual history has begun a slow death in American history departments, being displaced by "cultural history." Cultural history is driven by the fashionable theories of Foucault (1926-1984) and Derrida (b. 1930) concerning "knowledge/power," the post-Marxian notion that all thinking is a function of the power relations in a society. The cultural historians' project is not to discover what is good and true, or false and pernicious, in a given thinker's work; nor is it to assess how that thinker's work influences later developments of thought. Rather this project seeks to reveal the origin of a thinker's ideas in economic and other power relations. In this way a thinker's views are said to be "explained," rather in the manner of the historical critics of the Bible. But do we ever think of ourselves in this way? Does the cultural historian think of himself in this way? If he does not, and we do not, why ever would we think such a procedure would yield true understanding of the past?

Students also frequently encounter what we might term a "learning problem" in this course. Faced with great minds who appear to see through dearly held views such as those proposed by traditional religion, a student may feel the need to summon all his intellectual resources to refute these "masters of suspicion" in the most direct fashion, to smite them hip and thigh. Yet the same student may secretly fear that the "jig is up" on traditional faiths. For it is quite unlikely that even the brightest of students will be able to achieve anything approaching a demonstrative refutation of some of the world's greatest minds. Undergraduates should therefore focus their attention first on *understanding*—critically, of course. The best defense against unsettling texts is always to *read more*, and to read critically.

Moreover, if a core curriculum pursued in the spirit of Newman has taught a student anything, it should be that temporal parochialism is to be avoided; the most recent thinking is not necessarily the best. A clever and spare theory is also not the same thing as wisdom. And while each of the great nineteenth-century thinkers boasts of removing veils, dispelling illusions, revealing the unvarnished truth about the human condition, one may legitimately wonder whether these thinkers have broken through to new vision or merely propounded new myths. Intellectual equipoise is one of the great fruits of the liberally educated mind.

❧

Karl Lowith's *From Hegel to Nietzsche*, translated by David Green (New York, 1964; reprinted, 1991), is an elegantly written book describing the course of philosophy in the nineteenth century. Robert Nisbet's *Sociological Tradition* (New York, 1966; New Brunswick, N.J., 1993) and Raymond Aron's *Main Currents in Sociological Thought*, translated by Richard Howard and Helen Weaver (London, 1965; New Brunswick, N.J., 1998) both serve as valuable introductions to the sciences of man. Jacques Barzun's *Darwin, Marx, Wagner: Critique of a Heritage* (Boston, 1941; Chicago, 1981) offers judicious assessments. A sweeping religious perspective on such thinkers as Comte and Feuerbach is added by Henri de Lubac's *Drama of Atheist Humanism* translated by Edith Riley (London, 1949; San Francisco, 1995). In a more academic idiom, you may find useful James Turner's *Without God, Without Creed: The Origins of Unbelief in America* (Baltimore, 1985).

Concerning individual thinkers, Gertrude Himmelfarb's *Darwin and the Darwinian Revolution* (Garden City, N.Y., 1959; Chicago, 1996) places the father of scientific evolution carefully in the context of his time. Adrian Desmond and

James Moore's *Darwin: The Life of a Tormented Evolutionist* (London, 1991; N.Y., 1994) likewise contextualizes and demythologizes Darwin. Neither book is any sort of handbook refuting evolution, but both can contribute to your understanding of the topic.

Thomas Sowell's *Marxism: Philosophy and Economics* (New York, 1985) is an accessible introduction to the father of communist doctrine. Leszek Kolakowski's *Main Currents of Marxism,* translated by P. S. Falla (Oxford, 1978; reprinted, 1981), is the definitive work by an ex-Marxist theoretician. The writings of Alexander Solzhenitsyn are also valuable here.

That recent years have seen an explosion of work on Nietzsche is a bad sign, given the current politicization of the academy. Two recent thought-provoking exceptions are Fredrick Appel's *Nietzsche Contra Democracy* (Ithaca, N.Y., 1999) and Peter Berkowitz's *Nietzsche: The Ethics of an Immoralist* (Cambridge, Mass., 1995), though the latter may paint Nietzsche in colors too attractive.

Two good books on Freud are Frank Sulloway's *Freud: Biologist of the Mind* (New York, 1979; Cambridge, Mass., 1992) and Frederick Crews's remarkable collection, *Unauthorized Freud: Doubters Confront a Legend* (New York, 1998). Both are critical in the highest sense. Students should actively avoid the frequently assigned Peter Gay, *Freud: A Life for Our Time* (New York, 1988; reprinted, 1988), which is uncritical hagiography.

BEYOND THE CORE

TEN COURSES MORE

THE CORE CURRICULUM is the heart of the matter of undergraduate education. Indeed, as we saw with John Henry Newman, the nonelective, wide-ranging classical Western studies of nineteenth-century Oxford were once thought to be appropriately the whole of the college curriculum. Even as late as the 1950s, a student's core requirements frequently constituted more than half of his college coursework.

Today that is not the case, and you will eventually find yourself navigating through the many requirements of a "major" or "concentration." While presumably you choose your major based on personal interest and motivation, there are still common pitfalls to avoid. And quite often the right word of advice at the right time can prove to be the key that unlocks for you the inner logic of your studies. For expert guidance through your major, similar to that offered here for the core curriculum, the Intercollegiate Studies Institute is publishing a complete series of "Guides to the Major Disciplines." These monographs contain the personal reflections and advice of some of the country's most distinguished scholars. They distill insights gained in decades of award-winning teaching. These guides show you the way to get the most from your major.

Still, having completed the eight courses that here constitute a core of your own, you may find yourself with some remaining electives and a desire to explore the Western tradition further and for its own sake. If so, here are some suggestions for additional courses that can help complete your view of the Western *whole:*

Religion: *The Old Testament.* If your college offerings have constrained you to take a course on the New Testament rather than a course on the Bible as a whole, you really must proceed to the Old Testament. (Not to do so is to succumb to one of the oldest Christian heresies: Marcionism.) In the Hebrew scriptures, a fundamental Western paradox is first played out: the tension between the universalism implicit in Abraham's world-shaking discovery of the One God—monotheism—and the particularism of God's special covenant with and gift of the Law to his chosen people, Israel.

History: *Roman History.* The American founders looked to Greek history primarily for *cautionary* tales—examples of what can go wrong with republics. But in the Roman experience they found virtues and institutions that worked. It is no accident that so many of the early American pamphleteers took Roman names for their pseudonyms, the foremost being Publius, the collective pseudonym of the authors of *The Federalist* (Hamilton, Madison, and Jay).

Comparative Literature: *The "Divine Comedy."* This great epic has been called the *Summa Theologiae* set to poetry. The cosmic dimension of the Christian faith is made powerfully clear as Dante plumbs the depths of hell and then approaches "the love that moves the sun and the other stars."

Philosophy: *Introduction to Modern Philosophy.* For an alternative understanding of the nature of modernity, one that focuses on problems of knowledge and the metaphysical legacy of Christianity, you need to encounter such thinkers as Descartes (1596-1650) and Hume (1711-1776) and Kant (1724-1804), and here is where you will meet those minds at their best.

Political Science: *Constitutional Interpretation.* While America's founders set out to establish *novus ordo saeclorum*, a new order for the ages, they nonetheless took pride in upholding the continuity in America of the main body of English common law, a set of practices and judgments inherited from time immemorial. Regarding the most important things, wisdom is found not only in the minds of singular philosophical geniuses, but sometimes—perhaps more frequently—in the voice of tradition, "the democracy of the dead."

Economics: *History of Economic Thought.* Those drawn to the life of the mind often view business and economic production with lofty disdain. But since human beings are *embodied* spirits, "getting and spending" is no small matter. Economic policies can mean the difference between wealth and poverty for whole societies. And as the twentieth-century showdown between the followers of Adam Smith (1723-1790) and Karl Marx showed, economic systems can also mean the difference between liberty and tyranny.

History or History of Science: *Introduction to the History of Science.* The prestige of science in the modern world has come at the expense of philosophy and theology. Science was thought capable of an absolute knowledge unavailable to other forms of inquiry. To discover that science can have a *history* is to put science in a more humble but still important place. Scientists already know this. This course lets nonscientists in on that secret.

English Literature: *The English Novel.* The novel, the introspective prose epic of everyday life and ordinary people, is the dominant literary form of the modern world. Long after you have completed your last college course, you will continue to read novels for pleasure. Here can be found authors you will want to return to for the rest of your life. And to appreciate the work of the incomparable Jane Austen (1775-1817) is perhaps the surest sign of a civilized soul.

Art History: *Renaissance Art History.* Exposure to the paintings and sculptures of the most fertile period of artistic production in Western history will give you deeper insight into the classical and Christian themes that are the subjects of these works—and transform your experience of art museums for the rest of your life.

Music: *Music Appreciation.* This is the classic "gut" course, a favorite of seniors looking for light work. But this frequently well-taught course offers so much more. After experiencing the unparalleled achievements of Western classical music, you may be startled to discover that you can no longer listen to your stereo with the inattentive pleasure you could before. You will in any event be able to recognize precisely what it is you like or dislike about certain music. And you may recall—either with alarm or with satisfaction—that according to Plato, a proper musical education is the first step on the path to the health of the soul.

Even if you have stopped with our eight core courses and gone no further, you still have run the race, fought the good fight, and followed closely the course and contours of the West. You have struggled with some of the best which has been thought and said. You have been introduced to many alternative approaches to knowledge. You have seen questions raised that you did not know could be questions, and you have seen the dramatic differences various answers can make. You have seen that "what everybody knows" isn't always true. As you cross the finish line of the core curriculum, you perhaps will find yourself like Socrates, who could account himself wise only in that he was aware of his ignorance.

Perhaps. But if you have followed Newman's advice, thinking hard how to connect in your own mind all the disparate perspectives and fragments of knowledge you were acquiring through these courses, in wonder you may begin to realize that you do understand something about what is going on in the world. You will have acquired a philosophical habit of mind, and that is a human good that no one can take away.

The good news is that you now know something, not least, about yourself.

The even better news is that you will be able to learn more and more by assimilating new knowledge within an understanding of the Western *whole* which is now your permanent possession.

There is no bad news.

EMBARKING ON A LIFELONG PURSUIT OF KNOWLEDGE?

Take Advantage of These New Resources
& a New Website

The ISI Guides to the Major Disciplines are part of the Intercollegiate Studies Institute's (ISI) **Student Self-Reliance Project**, an integrated, sequential program of educational supplements designed to guide students in making key decisions that will enable them to acquire an appreciation of the accomplishments of Western civilization.

Developed with fifteen months of detailed advice from college professors and students, these resources provide advice in course selection and guidance in actual coursework. The Project elements can be used independently by students to navigate the existing university curriculum in a way that deepens their understanding of our Western intellectual heritage. As indicated below, the Project's integrated components will answer key questions at each stage of a student's education.

What are the strengths and weaknesses of the most selective schools?
Choosing the Right College directs prospective college students to the best and worst that top American colleges have to offer.

What is the essence of a liberal arts education?
A Student's Guide to Liberal Learning will introduce students to the vital connection between liberal education and political liberty.

What core courses should every student take?
A Student's Guide to the Core Curriculum instructs students in building their own core curricula, utilizing electives available at virtually every university, and discusses how to identify and overcome contemporary political biases in those courses.

How can students learn from the best minds in their major fields of study?
Student Guides to the Major Disciplines introduce students to overlooked and misrepresented classics, facilitating work within their majors. Guides currently available assess the fields of literature, philosophy, U.S. history, economics, political philosophy, and the study of history generally.

Which great modern thinkers are neglected?
The Library of Modern Thinkers will introduce students to great minds who have contributed to the literature of the West and who are neglected or denigrated in today's classroom. Figures who make up this series include Robert Nisbet, Eric Voegelin, Wilhelm Röpke, Ludwig von Mises, Michael Oakeshott, Andrew Nelson Lytle, and many more.

In order to address the academic problems faced by every student in an ongoing manner, a new website, **www.collegeguide.org**, was recently launched. It offers easy access to unparalleled resources for making the most of one's college experience, and it features an interactive component that will allow students to pose questions about academic life on America's college campuses.

These features make ISI a one-stop organization for serious students of all ages. Visit **www.isi.org** or call **1-800-526-7022** and consider adding your name to the 50,000-plus ISI membership list of teachers, students, and professors.